Meredith, we're in!
Parts One & Two
"The Life Story of Fred Kitchen told by himself"

Meredith, we're in!
Parts One & Two
"The Life Story of Fred Kitchen told by himself"

Fred Kitchen

Copyright © 2013, Frederick Simon Kitchen-Dunn

All rights reserved. No part of this book may be reproduced, stored, or transmitted by any means—whether auditory, graphic, mechanical, or electronic—without written permission of both publisher and author, except in the case of brief excerpts used in critical articles and reviews. Unauthorized reproduction of any part of this work is illegal and is punishable by law.

The cover cartoon entitled "We're in" Fred Kitchen in the Bailiff, is by Tom Webster dated 1907. The two men were great friends and remained so for the rest of their lives. A second Tom Webster cartoon is used in the book and was for Fred's benefit, dated 1945. After Fred retired from the stage in 1945 the two continued to meet up at the Eccentric Club to chat about events of the day. This is an attempt to make contact with either Maureen Pritchett nee Webster or her sister Paddy. I hope that by using these illustrations it will keep the memory of both these great men alive. It is not my intention to infringe on anyone's copyright in any way. If you wish please contact me at frederickkitchen@gmail.com

ISBN: 978-1-291-00168-6

1st Edition
Published by Frederick Simon Kitchen-Dunn 2012
frederickkitchen@gmail.com
Printed by www.lulu.com

PROLOGUE

This is the tale of an "Old Pro," – one who was born and bred to the stage, and for over half a century has loved it, and lived for it, and by it, – sometimes prosperously, sometimes on the verge of starvation; one who has known intimately the Dramatic Theatre and Music Hall world when that world was at its best and brightest; who has numbered some of its most brilliant stars among his best friends, and has shone in it as a star himself.

* * * * *

When I was six weeks old I was carried on to the stage at the Theatre Royal, Portsmouth, to take part in the christening scene of that moving melodrama "The Dumb Man of Manchester," and when I was nearly sixty I acted in a film whose hero was the famous greyhound, Mick the Miller.

The story I have to tell is of some of the happenings that lie between those two widely separated and strikingly different performances.

Chapter I

My father was Richard Henry Kitchen, but for stage purposes he was just R. H. Kitchen, comedian, pantomimist, and one of the finest clowns and harlequins of his time. He spent his whole life on the stage, and a long life it was. In his day children were apprenticed to actors, it was the only way onto the boards; and my father was apprenticed to Mr. Frampton, at what is now universally known as The Old Vic. Then it had the rather more dignified title of The Victoria Theatre, Waterloo Road. My father eventually reached the topmost rank of his own particular ladder, and it is to him I owe all the training in stagecraft and technique which since has served me so well.

My mother, Elizabeth Burry, owned a unique business which had been in the family for generations, indeed centuries. It dated from the time of James I, and was in fact created by that monarch.

It happened that one fine day the King was walking through his royal park, when he came across a pretty milkmaid milking one of the cows then allowed to graze there, and, being ever susceptible to a comely face, he stopped and begged a mug of milk. The maiden blushed, but she milked the cow there and then, and handed His Majesty his drink with such grace and charm that, thereupon, he promised to confer on her and her heirs for ever the ground on which they stood, and the right to sell milk and rusks there, to whomever wished to buy.

He kept his word and a stall was erected, and later a part of St. James's Park was enclosed. My mother was a direct descendant of that fair maid. Right up to her death in 1915 you might still have seen a cow tethered in the Park, and if you wished you might have taken a drink of milk fresh from nature, even as King James had done.

There were times, naturally, when the authorities suddenly woke up, rubbed their eyes, and wondered if something couldn't be done about it.

When the Queen Victoria memorial was planned, for example, there was an attempt to bring this ancient monopoly to an end, but my mother wrote to King Edward. The result of this was that His Majesty graciously granted us an alternative plot of land in the Park, in respect for the memory of the Stuart King, and, moreover, built a large sort of chalet, which existed until a few years ago.

As a youngster I used to drive our cows to and from the Park, deliver milk to members of the aristocracy in Carlton House Terrace, and generally make myself useful to mother in this business of public catering of which she was so fond.

Many people to-day will no doubt remember my mother and her sister, who were the last to maintain this ancient privilege of our family. No-one but had a kind word for her, and there was no-one to whom she, in her turn was not kind and charming. She was a first-class business woman, and at times made a considerable amount of money, but she shared with us of the stage a trait which is one of our marked weaknesses - she couldn't

The Burry Family

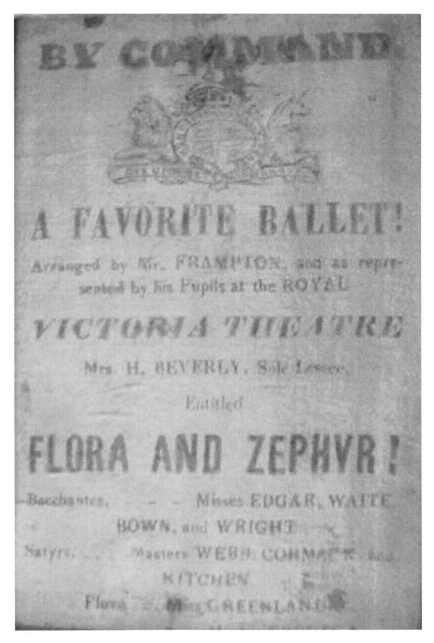

By Royal Command - R H Kitchen as one of the Satyrs

keep her money when she'd made it! She had a business head but not a business heart, and she always wanted to give her money away, usually to hard-up "pros".

My father, on the other hand, was lost away from the stage, and the only occasion on which he tried his hand at making "big money" outside it ended in disaster.

It was just after the Egyptian campaign of 1882. Things had not been going too well with the Kitchen family at the time, and when it was announced that Queen Victoria had promised personally to pin the medals on the breasts of the returned soldiers in a great parade on the Horse Guards, it looked like a good chance for us.

The month was November and my father was disengaged, awaiting Christmas and the pantomimes, and he decided to take part in this promising enterprise.

"The people don't want sponge-cake and lemonade and ginger-beer in November," he said to my mother. "They want barons of beef, and saveloys. Leave it to me..... And we'll build a grand-stand too, and charge a guinea a head for seats. People will always pay to get a good view of the Queen. It will be on our own ground, and nobody can say us nay."

So off went Father down to the New Cut, where he dropped in on a butcher called Quartermaine. Mr. Quartermaine agreed to supply an adequate number of rounds of beef, and some hams, and huge piles of saveloys. And a builder not far away undertook to build the grand-stand. Yet another firm got orders for tables, while the catering firm accepted orders for urns of coffee and tea to put on them, accompanied by long sandwich rolls and cutlery and the like.

Most of the family were in the park the night before the big day, working until dawn, only there was no dawn!

That day produced one of the worst November fogs it has ever been my lot to experience. The ceremony was postponed, and the Queen decided that whenever it was held it should be under cover. And under cover it was, weeks later, at the Agricultural Hall!

What Mother said to Father! And what Father said to Mother!

The position wasn't improved when the butcher and the caterer both refused to take back the edibles. I think the Kitchen family and their friends lived on beef, ham and saveloys for weeks! And all that while the builder and the people who had supplied the urns and sundries were never off the doorstep.

It took Mother, I think, about eighteen months to recover from that little effort of Father's to make money outside his beloved stage.

My parents' marriage was an ideally happy one, but Father often told me that if it had not been for the waywardness on one occasion of a certain white horse he might never have married my mother!

It happened like this: Frank Huntley, father of the famous G.P., was a great friend of my father's, and they frequently played together. Each had a sweetheart, and often in the summer the four of them would spend Sunday together, making a picnic of it, or going to some place of local interest for the day.

Now, my father was one of the few men who ever played Mazeppa. It is a part, of course, usually played by a woman; the character was indeed "made" by Miss Ada

Isaacs Mencken; but Father was one of the most versatile people of his day, and no part came amiss.

As everyone knows, Mazeppa in the famous play is bound to "the wild horse of Tartary," a beautiful white steed, which then dashes with his helpless burden over the rocks, or, as the play itself has it: "once more he urges on his wild career."

Well, for one of these pleasant afternoon foursomes, father borrowed the "beautiful white steed," hired a trap from a local butcher, and they set off for a picnic in a distant beauty-spot.

Arrived there, they took the horse out of the shafts, unloaded the victuals, and proceeded to have a happy little party.

But they had not counted on that "wild horse of Tartary." He was not an ordinary horse, and he had his own ideas about being wild and enjoying himself. So, when the time came to be getting back to the theatre – alas! No horse!

At last they found him – buried to his middle in a swamp of sticky, nasty, slimy mud.

Somehow they got him out, but, alas! for the beautiful white coat that had qualified him to play in "Mazeppa." There he was, plastered with filth. They tried bits of hard stone, old pieces of barrel-hoop, anything they could find about, but all the scraping in the world wouldn't remove the mess in the time they had for the job.

That night the beast went on looking nothing at all like the beautiful white steed described in the programme, but white on top only, and for the rest such colours as you might see at the bottom of a dried-up ditch.

That was funny enough, but I don't suppose my father would have remembered it if it had not been for the consequences, for the result was that the sweethearts quarrelled over whose fault it was, and there was a very strained atmosphere for a while. Then it cleared away, behold! The couples had changed partners! My father had proposed to Frank's sweetheart, and Frank had proposed to Father's girl.

Soon afterwards the exchanged sweethearts married.

Now, here is a pretty problem: If that horse hadn't wandered away that day, would I have been G.P.? And would G.P. have been me?

* * * * *

I was six years old when I had my first engagement in pantomime. Since then I have played in more than a score of them, but I doubt if I have ever got more kick out of any first appearance than I did out of "Little Red-Riding-Hood, Bonny Boy Blue, and a Little Old Woman Who Lived in a Shoe," as that pantomime at the Imperial Theatre, adjoining the old Royal Aquarium at Westminster, was rather elaborately called.

The Imperial was then under the management of Miss Marie Lytton, who surely must have been one of the first actress-managers, since she was as famous an actress then as she was efficient as a manager.

My father had been engaged to produce the show and the cast, I remember, included the late Lionel Brough, who played Johnny Stout.

Those pantomimes were wonderful things. No pains were spared to provide realism. I recall that on the stage of the Imperial there was a big farmyard scene in which we had real animals – real geese and hens and turkeys and pigs and pigeons, and even one of my mother's cows from the famous Kitchen fresh milk stall in St. James's Park.

And the cow was paid fifteen shillings a week for her services!

This pantomime was the only time when so many members of my family worked together in one show at the same time.

My father played the wolf, my sister Lisette played Little Boy Blue, my brother Richard the Demon (and he also worked the star traps which are seldom seen nowadays), and I was the farmer's boy in the first part and Little Billy Burley who was discovered in bed by the Old Woman Who Lived in the Shoe in the latter part.

In the cast also was the late Paul Martinetti, a French Canadian who was a very able and popular clown and head of the famous Martinetti troupe. Martinetti is still remembered affectionately for his work in many of his well-known sketches, such as "A Duel in the Snow," "A Terrible Night," and "Robert Macaire," in which he played Jacques Strop.

As I have said, Martinetti was engaged to play Clown. But he did a fire scene in the Harlequinade which was so realistic that it frightened the children in front, and the management cancelled his contract and engaged in his place a clown named Harry Paulo, an excellent clown in his day, and one of the wittiest and most amusing characters it has been my lot to know.

I remember well a story my father used to tell of him which he called "The Battle of Waterloo."

"The real Battle of Waterloo," he would say, "was fought in the Waterloo Road between 'Napoleon' William Molesey and 'Wellington' Harry Paulo."

Molesey's particular line, I must explain, was to impersonate Napoleon on the stage. Dressed in the famous Napoleon hat and the Napoleon coat he would sing straight stuff, including one song which was always a sure hand-getter, and which went like this:

"When I have conquered England
I have conquered all the world!"

At the time of this incident he had been impersonating the illustrious Frenchman so long that he had really come to imagine that he was the great Napoleon. (I have found that it often gets them that way. There must have been just "that little extra something" about Nap!).

It was one of Harry Paulo's very hard-up days and, strolling along the Waterloo Road, he looked into the public house called "The Hero of Waterloo," which incidentally was the terminus for a little bus service which a good many Londoners will remember – the bus that for the modest sum of one halfpenny would carry passengers from The Hero of Waterloo to Trafalgar Square.

It had no conductor; one just dropped the ha'penny into a box, or, if change was required, pushed up a little window behind the driver, punched him in the back, handed him the coin, and he gave you the change all done up in a little packet.

When, that day, Harry Paulo looked into the bar of the "Hero," whom should he see but Molesey standing all alone having a drink at the bar. For some unknown (or at least unrecorded) reason Molesey hated the sight of Paulo;

but hope springs eternal, it was a hot day, and Paulo was thirsty, and perhaps he thought that Molesey might, as they say, "push the boat out." So he gave him a pleasant "good morning."

It was a vain hope. Molesey merely turned around, looked Paulo right in the face and replied: "Don't you speak to me, Paulo. I don't want to know you."

Not unnaturally, Harry Paulo lost his temper.

"Oh, I suppose you think you're b— Napoleon, do you?" he retorted. "Well, I don't think you are Napoleon. I think you're a — — —!!!!" - and gave him a mouthful.

The landlord, hearing this and fearing the inevitable sequel, immediately came round to the front of the bar and said: "Here, that's quite enough of that in this bar. If you want to quarrel, get outside."

Paulo turned to the landlord and enquired: "Well, do you think he's like Napoleon? He thinks he is Napoleon."

"I don't care who's Napoleon or who's Wellington. This is the Hero of Waterloo and I ain't going to have any b—- battle here. So out you go."

And he shoved them both, willy-nilly, out into the street.

By this time Molesey was very indignant, to put it mildly. He turned to Paulo, placed his hat on in the Napoleonic manner, stuck his hand in the breast of his jacket, stared Paulo in the face and said: "Never you speak to me again. That is the first time I have been turned out of a public house."

"And remember, Harry Paulo," he added with fine dignity, "I am the only representative of the great Napoleon!"

Instantly Paulo replied: "Then, Gawblimy, I must be the Duke of Wellington," and crashed his fist into Molesey's face, knocking him down.

And just as he fell one of the little ha'penny buses was moving off and Paulo added: "And now come on. Have a ha'path over the bridge as far as Trafalgar Square. I'd like Nelson to see you!"

* * * * *

Harry Paulo, as I have said, was an excellent clown in his day, so good in fact that he was always willing to take risks for his effects.

Even during that pantomime at the Imperial when he took Martinetti's place, an accident occurred which might easily have finished his career for good.

He did a scene "on the roofs" with the face of Big Ben in the background, and when chased by a policeman had to run up the roof and do a spectacular leap through the face of Big Ben, being caught behind in a kind of hammock.

At one corner of the hammock was a rope with a running noose which kept the hammock taut, and after Paulo fell into this, the man guarding the rope had to let it slide down and thus lower the clown to the stage.

Not unnaturally, it was a custom for artistes who took part in dangerous trap work to give an occasional tip to the stage hands who looked after their tricks, but Paulo, although ordinarily a generous one, had taken a dislike to the particular hand who should have been looking after him and had declined to "grease the rope," as it was eloquently termed.

One night, on leaping through Big Ben's majestic face, he landed in the hammock all right, but the man who should have been there was missing, so that poor Paulo crashed, hammock and all, about ten feet down to the hard stage, and broke his leg.

He was hurried out of the theatre into a cab and rushed to Westminster Hospital, which fortunately was quite near, and on being carried into the ward smiled through his clown's make-up at one of the pretty nurses and said cheerfully: "Hello, here we are again – but they've brought me to the wrong dressing room."

Harry was a very generous man.

One day I met him in the same Waterloo Road and he was speaking to an old lady whom I had forgotten but who remembered me as a child. She was at one time a big star at the old Marylebone Theatre, but had since fallen on hard times.

Paulo at the moment had nothing to give her, but he suddenly remembered a new set of false teeth he had.

Telling the woman to wait a minute, he dashed across the road to the pawnbroker's that stood next to the old churchyard, and pawned his teeth.

A minute later he was back and gave the woman ten shillings – which was just like him.

How Harry Paulo came to possess those good and pawnable false teeth is interesting, too.

It was the time when the late Edward Terry was playing "Sweet Lavender" at Terry's Theatre. Edward Terry was a very kind man, but he didn't like giving money to importunate people who might stop him, as many did, and ask for the loan of say half a crown or five shillings.

But this he would do: if the applicant happened to have anything wrong with his teeth which might prevent him getting an engagement, Terry would give him a card to go along to a first-class dentist and get them attended to, or to have a new set made.

He one day met Harry Paulo – Harry, I have not the slighted doubt, had stopped him with the usual request – and Harry told him that he could get an engagement, but "it was so awkward having lost his teeth." Whereupon out of the kindness of his heart, Mr. Terry gave Paulo a card so that he might go to the dentist.

Paulo went, and eventually the new teeth were made. It was not so long after this that the two met again.

"Well, how are the teeth, Paulo?" Terry asked.

"I don't know, sir," said Paulo.

"How do you mean, you don't know? You've apparently got the teeth in. If there's anything wrong with them you must take them back and have them put right."

"Oh, the teeth are all right," Paulo said, "but, you see, Mr. Terry, I haven't been able to try them yet, because I've got nothing to eat!"

This amused Edward Terry so much that he broke his rule and gave Paulo five shillings to get something "to try his new teeth on." He used to say later that the story was well worth both the cost of the teeth and the five shillings, he had told it so often.

Chapter II

When I was a small boy the paternal Board of Trade Act, which for some years now has restricted the employment of juveniles, either on the stage or elsewhere, did not exist, so that long before I even went to school I had been playing child parts, whenever my father or my own good luck gave me the opportunity. Even after I started attending school my so-called "education" was much interrupted by stage engagements.

Sometimes in my earlier years my mother would give me lessons out of a spelling book, but when I was about eight my parents decided I should go to school, and I was packed off to a "seminary" in Hercules Buildings (now known as Hercules Road), off the Westminster Road.

At the back of the school were the Archbishop of Canterbury's grounds, now partly built on and partly a public recreation ground. On the same side of the bridge are Lambeth Palace and Lambeth Palace Church, where both my father and I were christened.

There must have been about two hundred boys at the school at the time. A very large proportion of them were sons of people connected with the 'boards'. Among them were many who have since risen to considerable heights in the profession. Names that recur to me, for example, are Arthur Rigby and his brother

Charlie Paton (whose real name, incidentally, is 'Turner'), Arthur Reece and his brother, Vesta Victoria's brother, Lawrence Barclay, and Clay Smith, who went to America and then returned to this country with Lee White and Percy Honri.

The headmaster of the school was one Doctor Herniman, one of the finest specimens of a Scotsman I have ever known. He stood well over six feet, had big, massive broad shoulders, a long black beard almost down to his waist, and, to finish the picture, he always wore a Balmoral bonnet.

Dr. Herniman was a great disciplinarian. When any of the boys met him in the street he had at once to stand to attention and salute, but, in spite of his stern discipline, he was a kindly-disposed, big-hearted man, and, irksome as I found school, I loved the doctor.

During my time at school I remember we had a new master, and the day he arrived I went to school wearing a red wig I had found among my father's props.

The master, not knowing of course that I hadn't been born with hair that colour, saw nothing wrong, but perhaps it was too much to expect the rest of the boys at school to stand for it. They laughed and they giggled at the most awkward moments, and at last the master realised that something was not as it should be.

Even then, though, I should have got away with it (though perhaps I would have had to be ginger-headed the rest of my school life!) but that one of them, in passing me, deliberately knocked the wig off my head.

That settled it. I draw a merciful veil over the sequel.... It occurred the following morning when, after prayers and in front of the whole school, the daily thashings took place.

And I might add that it was not the only time I played a leading role in one of those knockabout entertainments. Those were the days when they did not believe in sparing the rod.

There was a youngster named Dibsdale, whom I liked very much. We became inseparables. He was two or three years older than I and perhaps for that reason was able to put me up to more mischief than I could have thought of by myself.

So, one day, I remember when we had received from our respective fathers the sixpences which were to pay for the week's schooling, he suggested – and I must say I agreed readily enough – that we should put them to a far, far better use.

He waited for me in the morning and we met in the usual way and turned towards school, but we went not there. We went instead, down to the place where Doulton's now stands – a place where horses still can be stood in the Thames by humanely-inclined carters and waggoners – and where two or three barges in those days were moored.

Here we undressed on one of those barges and, amid the dead dogs, and the stench and the refuse that then added their peculiar piquancy to the Thames water (and, for all that I know, still do now,) we disported ourselves for the day.

But tomorrow came. As I remember it now after all these years, we weren't so keen by this time on our bathing, but we weren't keen to go back to school either – no longer having the sixpences. And in the end we had no choice but to make a week of it.

Then would come the following Monday ... and the sixpences again... and we were both afraid to go to school....

It might have gone on for ever, but at long last I summed up my courage, confessed the awful truth to my father, and he, understanding man that he was, took us along to old Dr. Herniman and told him some tale that saved our bacon.

This business of attending school was one of the difficulties of trying to acquire an education and at the same time attend the theatre. It led to all sorts of trouble and I remember well one hilarious incident when my father, worried by the calls of a too-inquisitive but not too polite School Board inspector, got his own back neatly.

As used to be the popular custom, the date of my birth and those of my brothers and sisters had all been ceremoniously entered on our arrival in the world in the Family Bible.

Now, we had a big black retriever dog, the pet of the family, and one day, pet or no pet, that dog amused himself by consuming quite a large part of that Bible – including the all important fly-leaf.

Shortly afterwards came one of the School Board men. Father went to the door and asked him what he wanted.

"Why hasn't your son Fred been to school?" the man enquired, not too courteously

"Why should he go to school?" asked Father.

"How old is he?"

"How should I know? Ask him!" And he pointed to the dog sitting contentedly beside him.

"What d'you mean – ask him?"

"Well, he's got the Bible inside him, with the date of his birth. So how should I know how old the lad is? Don't come here worrying about my boy. Go and see Charlie Paulo – he's got a boy, and he doesn't go to school."

And that was all the satisfaction the inspector got so far as I was concerned. But he went along to see Charlie Paulo – an old trouper of the Canterbury music hall – then a very old man.

Mr. Paulo came to the door.

"I hear you've got a son who is not attending school."

"Yes. Well, what about it?"

"Why not?"

"Better ask him yourself." And he called out, "Alfred!"

And out came Alfred. Alfred was a man of fifty-two, with a big black beard!

School days with me were far from popular, and an excuse for dodging them only too welcome; so when, walking home from school one morning, I was stopped by a stranger who asked me: "Are you Dick Kitchen's son?" I saw immediately a possible escape from school discipline and answered readily enough, "Yes, sir." I don't suppose I was very shy about it, either, - I wasn't that sort.

He told me he wanted a little boy about my size to play page-boy in a sketch he was doing. I jumped at it, especially when he offered me the immense sum of eight shillings a week!

For this munificent remuneration I was to play three halls – Weston's (now the Holborn Empire, and before that the Royal Holborn), the Bedford at Camden Town, and the old Marylebone music hall.

My employer worked a team with a lady named Beatrice Toye – a well-known name in the theatrical world

– as Romeo and Toye. I remember that sketch well, for I played what was probably my first real comedy part.

It was the old story of the music teacher and the aristocratic lady who comes to him for lessons. I was the page who showed her in, and sat on a stool in the music room while the lesson went on – making the irrepressible remarks that page-boys will, and having things thrown at me and tumbling off the stool and all that sort of comedy business. I enjoyed it!

"Romeo" (his real name I have forgotten now) used a hired brougham to take us from hall to hall, and at night when he had finished the last of the three shows, he and Miss Toye would drop me at the corner of Oakley Street, where we then lived.

I used to travel with my page-boy's uniform in a small tin box, and after the brougham had driven away, so proud was I of all this, that I would put on my little page-boy pea-jacket, resplendent with buttons, and my tall hat with its gay cockade (with about two editions of a Sunday paper inside the lining of the hat to make it fit me!) and make up again as best I could in the street, and then swagger home in pride and triumph, to make a dramatic entrance into the family circle!

Speaking of Weston's, I remember that in those days I was not honoured with a dressing room. I had to dress in a wine-cellar beneath the hall ... I wonder if they'd let me dress in a wine-cellar now!

There was a curious thing about the Marylebone music hall, too, with which I was then making my first acquaintance.

To reach the dressing room there, performers had to pass through the audience, and they had to do the same again when leaving the theatre.

It was sometimes embarrassing for the departing artistes, but more often for the turn then on the stage, for if you had pleased them, the audience, seeing you in their midst, would be sure to give you an ovation then and there, holding up the turn on the stage while you passed through.

While I was still playing in this sketch my father produced at the Victoria a comic ballet called "Dame Trot and her Comical Cat."

The "Vic" was then under the management of Miss Conns, and I remember that just about this time she engaged a new private secretary, a young lady of much charm and talent and ability. That young lady was Miss Bayliss, who since has done so much in connection with the revival of the Old Vic and Sadler's Wells.

It was at the Old Vic in this show that I first met the great comedian Little Tich, who was playing the Cat.

Tich, whose real name was Harry Ralph, came from Gravesend, where as a boy he used to play a tin whistle in the streets of the town for a living.

He was engaged to play Cat in my father's ballet, but in addition to this he also did a single turn, blacked up, calling himself then The Infant Mackney after a great negro performer of an earlier decade. During the run of the show The Infant Mackney managed to get himself a provincial engagement and he asked father to release him, which father did.

It was about the time of the famous Tichborne case and young Ralph thought he might get a little extra publicity by taking advantage of the fact. He therefore dropped his earlier names and now called himself Master Tichborne. I did not meet him again until three years later, when I was taken by my father to Liverpool to play "The Little Old Man of the Catskill Mountains" in that good old favourite "Rip Van Winkle," produced as a ballet divertissement.

On the bill, in addition to the ballet, there were five or six turns, one of them my old friend who had now changed his name again and called himself Little Tich. That was the first time I remember him with that title and the quaint long boots that were later to make him so famous.

Years afterwards I met Little Tich again in the pantomime "Humpty Dumpty" at Drury Lane, and again in Paris when Tich was the greatest English music hall star whom Paris had seen, and was appreciated and fêted as such.

M. Sacha Guitry paid a great compliment to Tich when he told a friend of mine that he thought that Little Tich, second only to his own father, was the greatest actor he ever saw.

As Mr. C. B. Cochran relates in his autobiography, M. Lucien Guitry, too, thought very highly indeed of Little Tich and, I am proud to say, of me. When he came to England, and was met by Mr. Cochran, he remarked that Little Tich and I were the best comedians he had ever seen, and asked where he could see us. That week I was playing at the Metropolitan Music Hall and Mr. Cochran came over to tell me of M. Guitry's generous tribute.

* * * * *

While I was still about nine years old, my father was engaged to play Clown and arrange the ballet in a pantomime at the old Alcazar Theatre in Holborn, which was later to become the Central Hall and later still the Stadium Club. Here we had an experience which I honestly believe to be unique in modern theatrical history.

The show ran for a whole fortnight without a licence from the Lord Chamberlain, and in deliberate defiance of the police.

The manager of the theatre was a man named John Baum. The pantomime was Cinderella, and the Demon King was played by the great Shiel Barry, famous as the original Gaspard in "Les Cloches de Corneville."

Structural alterations had been made in the building a month or two before, and in due course the usual and necessary licence was applied for from the Lord Chamberlain. This, however, was very firmly refused as the Board of Works reported that the staircase and balcony were unsafe.

Mr. Baum pleaded. If he did not open, he said, three hundred people would be thrown out of employment, and finally he was visited by the police and informed that (as a newspaper reported when the case came into the Courts later) "if the theatre was opened a body of police would not be sent down to make arrests, but subsequent proceedings would follow."

Still, the producer had gone on with the arrangements, hoping that at the last moment something would be done, even begging the aid of the Prince of Wales, who at that time took a keen interest in the theatre.

This went right on up to Boxing Day, the cast being ignorant of the position. The theatre had been beautifully decorated. It was the first time I had seen such plush seats and Brussels carpet in the 6d and 9d parts of any theatre.

Then, while, at the last moment, the fate of the show still hung in the balance, the queues were waiting outside for the doors to open for the first matinee, Mr. Baum extracted from the Prince of Wales a promise that he personally would see the Lord Chamberlain and try to obtain the necessary permission to open.

It was enough for Mr. Baum. Rushing round to the back of the theatre, he said: "It's all right, boys, we can open." And open we did.

And, moreover, we stayed open for two weeks, still hoping that we should get the licence. But it never came and finally the Lord Chamberlain closed us down.

Legal proceedings followed, but they came to nothing, for in any case Baum had no money left. He had lost everything he possessed in the failure of the pantomime.

Incidentally, that was the first time I remember in which the treasury failed (though by no means the last!) My father received his first week's money, but when the second week's treasury day came and he went along to collect, Mr. Baum said, "Oh, Mr. Kitchen, yours is rather a large amount and we haven't quite finished paying off the girls. Would you mind coming back a little later...."

And that was the last of that.

There is another little story about that ill-fated pantomime at the Alcazar which I must tell.

In those days it was the custom – not strictly orthodox, of course, but winked at by managements – for the clown to make a little bit on the side by mentioning local tradesmen from the stage. Usually he would pick up quite a few useful guineas doing this, the usual fee being two guineas a "mention."

I remember that one of his "customers" in this particular show was the manufacturer of a wonderful new musical instrument, the latest invention of the moment. It was one of those musical boxes in which a strip of perforated paper runs through the instrument and plays a tune. It was a simple device – crude of course to us to-day (although I suspect it might have been the father of all the barrel organs and the hurdy-gurdys) – and when the paper had run through and played its little melody it had to be removed, carefully rewound, and replaced in position to play again.

My part in father's little trick to earn his two guineas was to bring it to him on the stage, and he would say to me, "What's that you've got there, little boy?" and I would reply, "This is the latest invention in music, sir."

"Oh," he would say, "it's So-and-So's new musical instrument, isn't it?"

"Yes, sir."

"Give it to me, my boy. I will play you a tune on it. It's a lovely thing."

That was the idea. The rest is easy to guess. The temptation for me to try it out for myself in the dressing room had been strong – and I had fallen. And unfortunately, I had not understood about replacing the music-roll in position.

Dad did not get is two guineas that week!

And talking of this system of taking payment for blatant advertising on the stage, I remember a clown of a much later day, Harry Ewens, who was playing in pantomime at the Elephant and Castle Theatre. A

Mr. Upton, the famous hatter then by the Elephant and Castle, had given Ewens a guinea and a tall hat to advertise him.

This is the way we did it.

A boy would come on to the stage with a hat-box. The clown would take out the hat and try it on, and say, "Why, this is the best hat in the world. It must be from Mr. Upton, my boy," and so on.

All very well until Pantaloon got the bright idea that he ought at least to get a topper for himself out of it, too, even if the guinea was Clown's prerogative.

So Pantaloon, otherwise Harry le Mare, dropped in one morning on Mr. Upton with a visiting card and the polite suggestion, "How do I go for a top hat?"

"Nothing doing."

"Well, a bowler?"

Still nothing doing.

"Oh, come on, guv'nor, a new cap, then?"

But Upton was not to be cajoled and poor Pantaloon had to give it up.

That night, when Pantaloon and Clown were on the stage together, the little top hat act began.

"I think it's the best hat in the world," said Clown, according to contract, but Mr. Upton, if he was in the show that night, must have been staggered when Pantaloon knocked it off his head and cried, "And I think it's the worst I've ever seen."

Chapter III

After that tragedy of the Alcazar Theatre, back I went to my mother in St. James's Park, to mind the cows, deliver the milk, and sell gingerbread and cake.

Indeed, all my early life seemed to alternate between periods on the stage and intervals when I was chief assistant to my business-like mother. The stage I love; the ginger-beer merchandising I tolerated. My job was often to walk from Vauxhall Bridge to Carlton House Terrace, delivering milk and cream.

After delivering the milk I would walk back to Vauxhall Bridge and drive the cows to the Park. Then, on ordinary days, I would make myself generally useful about the stall, serving milk or chocolate, or ginger-beer.

Some days, when there happened to be a levee at the Palace, I would take a box of stone ginger and a pail of clean water and some towels, and walk along the Mall, supplying the coachmen with ginger-beer at 2d a bottle. There was a good profit in that, for we made our own ginger-beer, and it cost us about 1d for five bottles.

I got up to some tricks, too. When, for example, there was a review of any sort on the Horse Guards Parade, I would borrow a couple of ginger-beer boxes, get down behind the crowd, and let them out for stands at 3d per person – about 4 persons to a box.

Then I would go away and watch from a distance for a policeman to come and move the people on. At the right moment I would rush in and seize my boxes, then dodge to another spot and do it all over again! I made a good many shillings pocket-money for myself that way.

About this time we had a libel case against the Daily Telegraph. It arose this way –

Our stable had to be cleaned out by 10 o'clock each morning. One day we were a bit late, and the inspector called before it was done. We were summoned.

The Daily Telegraph ran a story to the effect that "the old ladies of St. James's Park," as they were then affectionately known to thousands of people, had been summoned for having dirty stables, and implying, at least, that the milk they sold was dirty and impure.

Mother and my aunt started an action against them, and we had many eminent witnesses on our side, including members of the peerage whom we used to serve with milk, and in the end we won our case, obtaining £2,000 damages, - a very considerable sum for a case of that kind in those days.

Shortly after this I made my first professional acquaintance with the Canterbury music hall, of which my foster-brother, Arthur Tressider, was at the time manager.

I say "professional engagement," but perhaps one could hardly call it that, for it was merely a job as attendant at one of the stalls in the long entrance to the hall which had been laid out as a kind of fair-ground, with shooting galleries, Aunt Sally stalls and ring-boards. I was engaged at one of these ring boards – "Here you are. Three Rings a Penny; and every Stick you Ring You Have!" – for the magnificent sum of six shillings per week.

Six months I kept this job, and I must admit I liked it, not only because it gave me a chance to forget that I was a schoolboy, and believe myself a showman, but also because those nights I would see the stars of the day going into the theatre, and the spenders and the hangers-on and the stage-struck passing into the then famous Canterbury Lounge.

Many of the young bloods of the time frequented the Canterbury Lounge in those days, and I have often seen champagne flowing there like water.

Here it was that I first saw Hyram Travers, the original pearly king, and a very clever coster comedian.

Many years later, when poor old Hyram had fallen on bad times, I engaged him as agent in advance. He was really worth more than his salary for his humorous outlook on life and the funny stories he would tell.

I remember that he was once at a race meeting with a well-known variety agent who was rather fond of the bottle. Hyram, I may mention, was a total abstainer all his life.

During the afternoon's racing, the agent remarked to Hyram that it might be very interesting to run race horses. "Good idea," said Hyram, "and it would be a good advertisement for you."

The result was that, with Hyram's assistance, he bid for the winner of a selling race, and it was knocked down to him for £200.

After becoming the owner of the horse, he said to Hyram: "Well? What do I do now?" "Well, you leave him with the man who has been training him," said Hyram. "It will cost you about £3 per week" – I believe that was about the figure then – "and you must register your colours."

"What d'you mean, colours?"

"Why the colours the jockey wears when he rides."

"Well, what colours would you advise me to have, Hyram?

Hyram looked at his agent's very conspicuous teeth, and said: "Well, there's only one colour for you, - green and gold, the same as your teeth!"

In the days when the "Era" was a sixpenny journal Hyram used regularly to have a humorous advertisement on the back page, and directly people bought their papers on a Saturday the first thing they would look for would be Hyram Travers' funny ad.

Another story of Hyram's concerned a certain Jewish gentleman who owned a music hall which was burned down. Soon after the fire he took another music hall, and by a strange coincidence this also was burned down.

And some time after, he took over a large wooden building in a popular seaside town, renovated and redecorated it, and generally fixed it up in good style.

Hyram Travers was engaged for the opening, topping the bill at £40 for the week, which then was big money.

The Yiddisher gentleman, proud of his new enterprise, invited Hyram to have a look round the place. They solemnly inspected circle and stalls, dressing rooms and bar and all the rest, and then Hyram was asked to "Come outside and have a look at it from the street."

So they walked across the street and the proprietor and Hyram gazed admiringly across at the new theatre.

"Well, Hyram," said the proud owner finally, "how d'you think it will go?"

"Well," Hyram said quickly, "it should go very well. It's got a tar roof!"

And it went!

Much to my regret, my mother opened a newspaper and general shop in Chapter Street, off Vauxhall Bridge Road, and she decided I should help her in the new business. So, perforce, I ceased to be a showman once more and sold newspapers. (That surely, if I had only appreciated it at the time, was the real basis of my future success – for what great man today has not sold newspapers! Or, if he hasn't, he generally boasts that he has – it seems to be the most elementary qualification for fame!)

However, I was far from being an unalloyed success at the job itself, for my duties included delivering the papers, and my mother soon discovered that if she did not dispense with my services she would be in a fair way to lose all her Sunday paper customers. As one peeved old lady told her one day: "It was a Sunday morning paper I ordered, not an evening one!"

At this time, too, I distinguished myself a little in the racing world. We used to sell what were (and still are) called "specials" at 5/- and 2/6 a time. I would get them in the morning with the morning newspapers, steam them open with a kettle of boiling water, copy out the tips, seal up the envelope again, and then sell the information thus illicitly obtained to my friends at 1d a horse.

Somehow, I used mysteriously to pick a lot of winners as a boy, and was never without pocket-money!

Then I got an engagement to play in a pantomime with J. M. Jones – "the Jones Troupe of Pantomimists" – at the ill-fated Grand Theatre, Islington, of which the proprietor at that time was Mr. Wilmott.

The pantomime was "Dick Whittington." The principal comedian in the show was Walter Andrews, one of the best Scottish comedians I have seen, and Cat was little Freddie Farren, who is still producing dancers in the West End.

Altogether it was a brilliant cast, which made all the more tragic the disaster that was to take place a few days after the show opened. Among the players, for instance, were Arthur Forrest, Arthur Corney, Martin Adeson, and others whose names even then were household words.

We played three matinees and three nights to crowded houses, but when, on the Thursday morning, we arrived where the theatre had been the night before, alas! there was no theatre there. It had been burned to the ground!

A public subscription was raised, and everybody received their money for eight weeks, with the exception of the one or two lucky ones who were able to get another engagement. Someone playing in the pantomime then running at Bolton had fallen ill, and Martin Adeson was fortunate enough to fill in.

But his luck was out, too, as it happened, for after playing for a few nights at Bolton, that theatre was burned out also, and poor Martin was out of work again.

Which reminds me of a little incident that happened to Martin just afterwards.

He had run over to Manchester and thought he would go in and see a matinee at a pantomime playing in one of the Manchester theatres.

Presenting his card, as was and always has been the custom in the profession, he expected to be given a seat without any query, but, to his chagrin, the manager merely answered, "Not likely. You're not coming in here. You've burned down two theatres already!"

On the Sunday following the disastrous fire at the Grand, I was reading an account of it out of a Sunday newspaper to my mother, as we sat behind the counter in the shop, when suddenly there was a shout from my Dad from the shop parlour.

We rushed in to find the room in flames, and had it not been for the presence of mind of my mother shutting the shop door and those windows that were open, so cutting off the current of air passing through the room, I am afraid there would have been yet another disaster.

Even as it was, the shock of the fire affected my father seriously, and left him with his memory materially impaired. Nothing that happened the day before could he ever in the future recall, although, right to the end, he could remember and converse freely about events that had happened years previously.

This was a terrible blow to him and us, for it rendered him practically useless for the stage, and this was the greatest calamity that could overtake a man so active and so fond of his profession as he was.

Only once again did he appear in public, and that was when he went down to the Theatre Royal, Woolwich, to play clown on the benefit night of his old friend. Harry Paulo.

I was in front on that last night of his, and I remember how wonderfully well he worked. The old Pantaloon was one who had played Pantaloon to his Clown some forty years before – Bob Marchant, the brother of Fred Marchant the dramatist who wrote what I believe was the first "sensational" drama "Forsaken" – a thriller in which a boy, tied to a plank in a sawmill, was slowly drawn towards the horror of the revolving saw.....

Dad and Bob Marchant went on without any rehearsal and greatly entertained the audience for at least twenty minutes.

That was my father's last appearance before a public he loved and who loved him. It is indeed sad for an old pro. when it comes to this, but luckily for father he had his boys and girls still for a few years to occupy his affection, and up to the very end he was always our severest critic and greatest teacher. With him there was only one way to do a thing, and that was the right way.

Chapter IV

After the fire at the Grand Theatre, Islington, there came another spell when I was back in St. James's Park. But it was not for long.

Christmas soon came round again and this year (it was, I think, 1887) brought me an engagement with Mrs. John Wood at the Court Theatre, Sloane Square, to play Jibber, the Donkey in the fairy play "Little Goody Two-Shoes" written by Rosina Filippi and played entirely by children.

This play ran for eight or ten weeks and, so far as I personally was concerned, was chiefly remarkable in that was the first time my name appeared in the newspapers, a fact of which I was somewhat proud. True, it was only a couple of lines in very tiny type, but it was in two papers and it said that Jibber was played by F. Kitchen; I felt that I was well on the way to fame!

During this time my sister Lisette had married Mr. J. P. Sutherland, then running the Victoria Theatre, Newport, Mon., now known as the Lyceum. Lisette was the only one of my two sisters to go on the stage, and she had been a pupil of Madame Katti Lanner, one of the finest dance instructresses and ballet mistresses of her time, and was now a principal dancer in her husband's production.

Sutherland was producing a pantomime at the Theatre Royal, Dewsbury. I went down to play the Old Man of the Sea in "Sinbad the Sailor," but on the journey down got my hand crushed in the door of the train.

So instead of playing the Old Man, I had the much less inspiring job of selling programmes in the auditorium.

After a few months with my sister I again returned to the duties of driving the cows to and from St. James's Park, but with the next Christmas came my first real provincial pantomime engagement – at the Theatre Royal, Hull, the lessee of which was then the famous Wilson Barrett.

At this time my brother Harry was a "utility man" at the Princess's Theatre in Oxford Street, where Wilson Barrett was then playing in "Romany Rye," and in which another "utility gentleman" (and this may be news to my readers, for I doubt many other people than myself now living know it), was the man who afterwards became Sir Walter Gibbons.

In this pantomime at Hull, where I really began my pantomime career, I had to play the Bogey Man, work the star traps and leaps without a double – and in those days there usually was a double – play a much-knocked-about fat boy in a picnic scene, and finish up as Harlequin in the Harlequinade, and all for the handsome salary of £2 a week and find your own Harlequin costume.

However, it seemed pretty good to me then. I managed to send my mother £1 a week and still have a fairly good time on the balance; but one night my career nearly came to a sudden and inglorious end!

I was working the star traps when I stood too far down on the "table." The table, I must explain, is the small platform from which the performer is shot vertically through the trap from beneath the stage, and it is essential that he takes up his position in the centre of it with perfect accuracy.

This table is weighted with pulleys and weights exactly to balance the weight of the artiste doing the trap act, and there are half a dozen stage-hands there to give him the quick lift that will shoot him through the trap at the right moment. Two give the table a shove and there are two at each of the ropes on which the compensating weights are hung.

The two at the table lift, and the four at the ropes pull, with the result that the performer goes up with all the impetus that six-man-power can give. On the word "Go!" up shoots the table, he gathers himself for the shock, his head strikes the centre of the star-trap immediately above and – crash! he is through, to appear like some magic apparition in the air.

All very simple - when you know how. But anyone who thinks that playing in a pantomime is soft – especially when playing the trap scenes – might give a little thought when he next goes to see one.

Anyway, on this night I am speaking of I was not on the dead centre of that table, or else I bent my knees too much in readiness for the concussion of striking and opening the star trap above me, and instead of going gaily through it as I should have done, I struck the side of it and, as I passed through it, my knees caught the edge.

The force of that blow you can imagine when I tell you that with my knees I tore away the entire trap, ripping its six-inch screws right out of their setting and wrecking the whole contraption!

It hurt.

The doctor came round and dressed my wounds, but I could not go on that night again nor on the following night, and even to-day I still feel the effects of the injury to my left knee – and, oddly enough, generally at Christmas time and in the pantomime season.

As late as last year, when I was playing Dame in "The Babes in the Wood" at Birmingham, I had to have it massaged, and this was done for me by the trainer of the Birmingham Football Team, to whom I had happened to mention this little trouble.

In the early months of 1888 following the pantomime at Hull, my brother-in-law, J. P. Sutherland, produced a kind of miniature musical comedy entitled "The Lily of Trouville" at the Louvre at Earl's Court.

This was the time of the great French Exhibition at Earl's Court, and in the show I played the part of a French waiter. It was here that I first came to know G. P. Huntley, with whom I was destined to become such a fast friend. Another member of the cast was David James, Jnr., who was a son of the David James of "Our Boys" fame, which had a record run at the Vaudeville Theatre.

The James's real name, by the way, was Belasco, and they were related to the famous Belascos of the American stage. I have heard my father say that Belasco the prize-fighter, who was celebrated in the very early days of the prize ring, was also connected to the Jameses.

Others in the cast were Florence Lavender, and Stuart Robson, then a well-known baritone, twenty-four ladies of the ballet with my sister Lisette as principal dancer, and J. P. Sutherland as juvenile lead, with of course a number of minor parts.

We were doing three shows a day – at 2, 7 and 9 o'clock and the show ran seventeen weeks.

About Tuesday G.P. and I were, of course (though I don't know why I say 'of course' except that it always happened that way), broke. George was then, I think, making about £3. 10s a week, while I was getting 35s.

George would suggest – it being Tuesday – that we should pay a visit to my mother in the Park. But, without money, how were we to get from Earl's Court to St. James's? That was where G.P.'s genius began to show itself.

George, as I soon discovered, had found out that if you went through a sort of side entrance into West Kensington station on the District Railway – an entrance that had been constructed specially for visitors to the Exhibition – and if you used it often enough, you could maybe get to know the ticket-collector on the gate.

You could walk out of the exhibition entrance right into the station and pretend you were going out of the station and through into the street, and with luck the ticket-collector would let you through without showing a ticket.

So, so long as we could muster twopence between us, G.P. and I would go through the West Kensington entrance, dodge across to the opposite platform, board a train and eventually get to St. James's Park where, with the most innocent expressions we could assume, we would blandly give up two pennies to the collector.

We would then visit Mother in the Park and would get the money from her to go to Whitcombe Street and buy a steak at Steele's the butcher's; then we would take it back to Mother who would cook it for us in the park – so that at least we got one square meal now and again.

Then, the meal over, George would borrow five shillings from my mother, and I could generally get half-a-crown, and then we would make for the "Marble Halls" as the pros called the long bar at the Adelphi Theatre, owned by Gatti Brothers – a popular rendezvous of the profession in those days.

A few doors from this was the "Bun Shop" which we would also visit. This was then occupied by Mrs. Egerton, who afterwards made the American Bar at Lime Street, Liverpool so famous.

About five o'clock we would buy a penny ticket at Charing Cross Station, change at Earl's Court, go to West Kensington, cross over, and come back through the special exhibition entrance, putting it over our good friend the ticket-collector once more.

There was another fellow playing in the show who also used to go home between the afternoon and evening performances, and hearing how George and I "worked" it there and back for twopence, one day tried the same trick – but at his very first attempt he was caught and fined forty shillings. Perhaps that made up for what the railway company didn't get from us.

About a couple of months before the Exhibition closed, a Café Chantant was opened next door to the Louvre Theatre where we were playing.

Now it happened that a great friend of G. P. Huntley's had the engaging of the artistes for this Café Chantant. His name was Frederick Jessett, and, of course, as pals will in our profession, instead of engaging French artistes or English performers with proved French mannerisms or style, he put in all his own pals.

Among these were George Gray, who later made "The Fighting Parson" famous, and who sang one or two light comedy songs; G. P. Huntley, who sang some Irish comedy songs – I remember one of them so well for its very incongruity; it was entitled "Down went McGinty to the Bottom of the Sea," and the refrain went like this:

"Down went McGinty to the bottom of the sea;
He hasn't come up yet; so he must be very wet.
They say his ghost still haunts the spot until the break of day, Dressed in his best Sunday clothes."

For this show I remember that G. P. had a little difficulty about his wardrobe, but with his usual genius he solved it. George went along to have a little talk with a pal of his at the Lyceum and between them they smuggled out a coat and hat which belonged to Sir Henry Irving and which that great actor had used when playing in "The Lyons Mail." These "borrowed" props served nicely as G. P.'s costume for his comic Irish songs.

When the Exhibition closed at the end of the summer, "The Lily of Trouville" was transplanted to the Royal Aquarium at Westminster.

In passing, I might mention that the Aquarium was an aquarium in name only – I never saw any fish there in my life, except the fried fish in which the stage hands indulged between shows now and again – and the only tank I ever saw filled with water there was used by the Beckwith family, the famous swimmers and submarine performers and divers.

In connection with this I recall the strange medley of sounds one could hear from inside the Aquarium. It was, to say the least of it, a bit disconcerting sometimes when performing on the stage in the centre transept to hear, coming through none to faintly, the exhortations of the various side-show touts. Old Mr. Ridgeway, for example, the doorman to the Beckwiths.

"Have you seen the ladies in the water?
If you haven't seen them, you oughter!" he would cry every minute or two. This stirring rhyme he told me he had composed himself – and I believed him!

And in another part of the building was a side-show called "Eve's Garden," whence came the distant cry, "This way for Eve's Garden. A thing of Life is a thing of Beauty and a Joy for Ever. This way for Eve's Garden."

That was Nat Emmett doing his stuff.

Eve's Garden, I remember, was run by Mr. Wieland who, a few years before this, had the great Zaeo, the lovely woman aerial performer. His daughter, Mrs. Betty Davies, after her father's death, became an impresario, and I owe to her kindness some very excellent contracts I have enjoyed in later years.

Talking of the Aquarium, I should point out that this was part of the same building as the Imperial Theatre, and a visitor to the Aquarium could pay the extra and walk through into the theatre.

G. P. Huntley, David James and I, when not playing ourselves, would often go into the Imperial to see a matinee performance.

Just at this time an American mesmerist named Kennedy had the theatre, and during his act he would appeal for any member of the audience to come up on stage and be hypnotised.

I remember one day a nice-looking, quiet young fellow walking up on to the stage and being hypnotised by Kennedy, who gave him a broom and said, "Now, this is a banjo, and you will imagine yourself a Christy Minstrel, singing a Christy Minstrel song." And after a few magic passes of the master's hands, the young man obliged with "A little peach in an orchard grew, Oh, listen to my tale of woe."

That young man was Mr. George Robey, and I well recall how his performance amused us all.

During this time Robey got an engagement in the Aquarium himself as a comic singer, and I remember one of the songs he used to sing, which ran:

"He'll get it where he's gone to now."

Also on the programme with us was a wonderful marionette show – Barnard's Marionettes. They were stopped by the L.C.C., who said that marionettes were indecent! However, Barnard brought a case against the L.C.C. and won it.

Following Kennedy the mesmerist at the Imperial there came a "strong man" who called himself Samson, a little dark Frenchman with a large black moustache such as one always imagines on a French gendarme, but with really amazing muscles. Samson issued a challenge to the world, offering a large sum of money to anyone who could emulate his feats of strength.

Many were the "strong men" who came forward and took up his challenge, but whether successful or not, somehow they never succeeded in getting away with the award.

Among these were two Germans called The Brothers Marx, for instance, who, after they had demonstrated their own strength against Samson's, claimed that they had certainly won the prize. There were long and heated disputes on the stage and off it, but they did not win.

Then came an English "strong man" named Attila, the same who afterwards had a school of physical culture on Brixton Hill. He brought along a fine-looking young German named Sandow and issued a challenge on his behalf to beat Samson.

The event took place, and Sandow easily beat the Frenchman.

When Samson found himself defeated, he went mad with fury, and there followed such a scene as resulted in an uproar that practically cleared the theatre. It was terrific, and it brought so much publicity the following day in the newspapers and there followed so much discussion that in the end Samson was forced to admit his defeat, and Sandow became the champion strong man of the world.

While I was at the Royal Aquarium my brother Richard, who by now had become a famous variety star on the Continental stage and had been decorated by the Czar of Russia at Moscow for his performance as Harlequin at a big fête at the Czar's Palace, came to London with his partner Jack Osborne for a few weeks' holiday.

Charles Lauri had just opened at the Alhambra playing in a big ballet and also playing one of his pantomime sketches.

He was short of two people for his sketch, which was called "On the Roofs," and my brother and his partner obliged him by playing the parts during their holiday. When finally their vacation was over and they had to return to the Continent Lauri offered the parts to my other brother Harry and myself, and so we took their places.

It was about this time that Charles Lauri brought to the Prince of Wales's the famous play without words "L'Enfant Prodigue." It was a tremendous success, making a great deal of money for him.

In plays of this type, which are pure mime, the orchestra plays a more than ordinarily important part, and Lauri was particularly fortunate in having with him a pianist who was destined to become one of our greatest and most famous musicians – none other than Landon Ronald, afterwards to be honoured by the world and knighted by the King.

After the immensely successful run of "L'Enfant Prodigue" at the Prince of Wales's Theatre, Lauri decided to send it on tour, but so little was it understood or appreciated by the provincial audiences that he lost on the tour all that he had made with the play in London.

We were at the Alhambra for nine months and, besides playing in the sketch "On the Roofs," my brother Harry and I played also in two other sketches, "The Sculptor and the Poodle" and "The Sioux."

Then we went to Drury Lane for pantomime. It was Christmas of 1891 and I was now 18. The panto was the old favourite "Humpty Dumpty" and Harry and I took the places of the Brothers Griffiths, who previously had been at Drury Lane for years without a break, as the Demon Cat.

It was an excellent cast. There were Little Tich, who played Humpty Dumpty, Dan Leno as Queen of Hearts, Herbert Campbell as the King of Hearts, Fanny Leslie as King Dulcimar, and Marie Lloyd who was Princess Allfair.

It was a double harlequinade, with two clowns, and these important parts were played by Harry Payne, one of

Drury Lane's greatest clowns, and Charles Lauri, who was playing this part for the first time.

The prop my brother and I had to use made it very hard work. The head of the Cat was so heavy that it required two men to lift it on to us. I remember how I put one across my brother in connection with that.

I had seen the thing being made in the property room and Harry hadn't, so when, just before rehearsal, he asked me, "Which part will you be, Fred: the front or the hind legs?" I said quickly, "Oh, I'll be the hind legs, Harry!"

The size of this prop can perhaps better be imagined when I tell you that in one scene we "swallowed" Fred Walton, and Dan Leno had to cut a hole in our side to drag him out!

Dan Leno, let me say in passing, was a comedian for whom I, and indeed everyone who knew him, had not only the greatest admiration but also great affection. He and Arthur Roberts were, in their different lines of comedy, to my mind the greatest comedians the stage has ever produced.

I have sat in front and when the number board went up, have seen people look at their programmes and, finding that Dan Leno was the next turn, start to laugh before ever he appeared on the stage. That is surely the most wonderful tribute the public could pay to any comedian.

And Dan was such a kind-hearted, lovable little man. I have seen them lining up outside Drury Lane on Saturday nights and Dan on the step of the stage door handing out little packets – certain amounts for certain people – week after week. These people were mainly "old pros" and others who had fallen on bad times. All done in such a quiet, unostentatious way. No-one ever appealed to Dan in vain.

Such a lot have I seen of this kindness in the profession that I have often wondered if any other profession in the world can equal it in its big-heartedness and sympathy and kind generosity. Apart perhaps from journalism, I doubt it.

Of course there are two types of pro, just as I suppose there are two types of journalist, but I have always found that the mean actor is the exception rather than the rule. Perhaps it is that the stage develops the human side of character.

With regard to Dan Leno, I have always felt what a happy thing it was that he could break away from the clog-dancing which began his career, and which, I have always believed, had much to do with the final breakdown in his health and may quite possibly have had a lot to do with his tragically early death.

Dan was almost born in clogs. Before ever I met him or had seen him on the stage, I had heard my father say that Dan's father and mother, when playing in a sketch at the old Steam Clock Music Hall in Birmingham, used to bring the little Dan on to the stage in a carpet bag, open the bag and lift him out, and then Dan would do his clog-dance.

Only once was there any question of Dan Leno being the greatest clog-dancer of his day: this was when he danced against a man called Ward, and the latter was awarded the championship belt. There was a good deal of controversy, though, about this award, and two opinions as to whether Dan was really ever outclassed.

Chapter V

Many times during my career I have been asked whose work has influenced me most in life, and unhesitatingly I have been able to reply – the works of Charles Dickens.

Indeed, I have felt that I have Dickens to thank for a great deal of my success. In my youth his incomparable books were almost a bible to me, and since I was eight years old I have been reading and rereading them.

Dickens it was who taught me the superb and immensely effective art of combining comedy and pathos, laughter and tears, which without a doubt has been one of the major secrets of such success as my sketches have enjoyed.

And always, too, I have been grateful for the miracle of that combination of humour and charm which the great novelist created. It is the happiness that Dickens personally gave to me that I have tried to pass on in my own little way to the world.

I should think I have read the immortal story of the cricket match in Pickwick Papers fifty or sixty times. When I have felt a little low-spirited at any time, or lonely, in some not too comfortable digs, I have turned with delight to that cricket match, and read myself back to cheerfulness with the struggle between the All-Muggletonians and the Dingley Dellers. Then Mr. Jingle - what a marvellous character! I remember hearing my father say that he thought Mr. Jingle was the greatest character Irving ever played. My father, indeed, admired Irving as much as a light comedian as he did as a tragedian.

I could not have been more than eight years old when I had my first experience of playing in a Dickens sketch. It was a production of "Nicholas Nickleby" at the Crystal Palace, and I was entrusted with finding thirteen other boys to play with me as the schoolboys at Mr. Squeers' academy. I remember how I stood at the side of the stage and watched the death of Smike, and cried my eyes out. I still cry when I watch a well-acted death scene, even at the pictures.

It was in about 1892 that I paid my first visit to the Continent, where in later life I was to spend so many happy years and enjoy such a marked and delightful success.

I went with Lauri and his troupe to play in Brussels, at the Alcazar Theatre in two of our pantomimic sketches, "Puss, Puss," and "The Sioux." On the same bill with us, I remember, was the beautiful Mlle. Yvette Guilbert, whom I thought then was the most charming, delightful and versatile artiste I have seen on the stage.

Here in addition to my first taste of the Continental stage I got my first experiences also of continental life, and began to know the meaning of late nights and early mornings. Some very amusing times I had, for instance, at the local races.

These race meetings, I should explain, were not really meetings held under the official rules as we understand them in this country, but what were termed "flapping meetings."

Most of the jockeys – I should say nine out of ten of them – were English, and at this time I met jockeys who had been "warned off" from all over the world, as it was no trouble for any jockey to obtain a licence to ride at these "flaps" whatever crime he may have committed or been accused of elsewhere.

At this time I was getting only £3 a week from Lauri, and as out of this I felt it my duty to send some money home each week, naturally I had little left to go racing with. But that was easily overcome, for my jockey friends would get me a horse which I could lead into the paddock and so at least solve the problem of admission.

Even if there were no horse available, I could borrow a horse-rug, or a pail and brush, and walk in with the authority of a stable boy or head lad.

Once in the jockeys' room, they would hold a meeting to discuss the day's racing, and at time I would be sent out before a race to see what the betting was like. I would write down a list of the horses and prices, bring it back to "the boys" and often they would say, "Well, we'll win with that one!" As a rule "that one" was a ten or twelve to one chance.

Then they would club together and sometimes muster as much as 150 or 200 francs, to which of course I would add my little bit. At this time, this sum would make a total worth about £7 or £8 (with the franc at its old par value of 25 to the pound). I would then go out with the "bank" and try to get it on at the best possible prices. But as a rule I could not bet more than fifty francs at a time with these small Flemish bookmakers.

So by the time I had got on, say, the £8, the horse would be almost favourite, much to the astonishment of the owner. You can imagine what kind of race-meetings they were, for a matter of £7 or £8 to bring down the price of a horse from, say, ten to one to two to one or even money.

I could fill pages with stories of these little jockeys. They were indeed the funniest group of men I ever met, and sometimes, if an inferior rider among them was not able to hold in the horse that was not planned to win, and happened to let it run away with him, and thus beat the animal the lads had the money on, the language was something fearful!

I remember a little jockey who had been warned off in France. He was nicknamed Sparrow, a little, wizened, quaint, strange man. One night, sitting round with eight or nine of the other jockeys, in a little café near the Bourse which they called their training quarters, Sparrow had a brilliant idea.

"Has it struck you," he asked suddenly, "that if anything happened to any of us we should be chucked into a pauper's grave out here?"

They agreed it hadn't struck them.

"Now, my idea is," he went on, "why shouldn't we start a burial society among us? Say we start with ten francs each in the kitty and say five francs each a week, so that should anything happen to any of us, at least we should have a decent funeral."

They all saw the force of his argument and jumped at the idea. The burial society was duly and ceremoniously formed and they all paid up until they had the equivalent of some £20 in the fund.

Then Sparrow died!

It is the custom on the Continent for mourners to follow the hearse on foot, and at Sparrow's funeral it was an odd sight to see these jockeys, all in their Sunday clothes, ready for the ceremony.

The funeral was most elaborate. They had spent all the money out of the new burial club and the coffin was covered with flowers, and they started off, these little men, their faces serious and solemn, to pay their last respects to their old pal, Sparrow.

During the procession to the cemetery, however, one of them suddenly had a brain wave, and said to the man walking beside him, "Have you tumbled anything?"

"No, what?"

"Why, Sparrer's caught us. He knew very well he was going to 'tail 'em off.' It was his idea, starting the burial club. Suppose anything happened to you or me tonight? Where should we be? There's no money left in the kitty to bury us!"

The thought soon spread to the other jockeys, and as they followed poor Sparrow the rest of the way to his grave, the tone of conversation changed, and what they said about poor Sparrow....!

We remained in Brussels for eight weeks and then went on to Marseilles, where we played at the Alcazar Theatre, and there I had the pleasure of seeing some of the greatest pantomimists on the stage, including Le Flemant, Bernadini, and Rolfe, who incidentally was so much like me in appearance that I was frequently mistaken for him. Another pantomimist there who, I think, was the only one to visit London, was Severin, whom Lauri brought over to His Majesty's to play in "Marchant d'Habit," and I am sorry to say that he was not a very great success here.

At Marseilles I was playing a young midshipman in "The Sioux." It was a very smart make-up, and being rather a smart youth myself at the time, I seemed to be of almost embarrassing interest to the ladies of the port.

Every evening the boxes were occupied by the loveliest young women of the town and showers of bunches of violets thrown on to the stage would greet my entrance. And then I was still able to blush!

There was one young lady in particular.... But that is another story. One thing I can say about her, though, is that being half French and half Spanish she could be a little embarrassing!

So for two months I had a very pleasant time, and then the engagement at Marseilles came to an end and we had ten weeks' vacation until our next date in London.

But I for one had no particular desire to return to London for ten whole idle weeks. Nor was it necessary that I should, for, during this time my brother Richard had settled in Paris and had married a young Parisienne whose father and mother had a café-restaurant in the Rue Vielle du Temple.

Dick was fourteen years older than I and I suppose, as we met so rarely, he could hardly be blamed for regarding me still as a baby, although I was eighteen years old. At any rate, he had apparently told his young wife about his kid brother coming to Paris, and I daresay she formed an impression of a nice, innocent, blue-eyed little boy, and was charmingly anxious to meet me.

I am afraid I shocked her.

Needless, perhaps, to say, in the excitement and celebration of leaving Marseilles I missed the train, but I did manage to catch the next one where I was fortunate or unfortunate enough to fall in with a cheery group of Zouaves on leave from Algiers.

At the last stop before reaching Paris we all rushed out, as travellers will, for a final spot of refreshment, and, I regret to confess, were still knocking back absinthe when the train started. We rushed for it but were too late to make it properly and two of the Zouaves and myself travelled the rest of the journey between two coaches sitting astride the buffers and clinging for dear life to the ironwork.

I arrived in Paris smothered in dust and grease, still feeling the effects of the absinthe, and with the fez of one of the Zouaves cocked rakishly on the side of my head.

And that was how I greeted my new sister-in-law, who had expected to see – well, not that!

Dick was then playing at the old Moulin Rouge, and he invited me warmly to stay with him in Paris rather than go on to London with Lauri and the rest of the troupe, which I was delighted to do, for my brother and I had always been extremely fond of each other.

I may say indeed that we have always been an affectionate family, bound together not only by fraternal ties, but linked also by a common love of the stage which has been shared by every member of the family. Even my mother, although indeed she had no practical part in it – or hardly any, since she appeared on the stage only once in her life, and that not in any important part – shared my father's and her children's enthusiasm for the profession.

And it turned out luckily for both of us that I had remained in Paris, for while Richard was playing one night he fell, hurting his back and putting himself out of action for a while. So I stepped into the breach, took over his part for the rest of the engagement, and though perhaps, inexperienced as I was, my performance was far from being the equal of Richard's, at least I kept his end up and saved his salary.

Dick and his partner then went to Trouville for a month and I went with them. It was "the season" and we had a glorious time. Never since have I seen so many American and English millionaires gathered in one place. The harbour was gay with the most wonderful yachts, both English and American, and all society was on parade. And to add to my pleasures I even got a walk through the gaming rooms, but that was only in the daytime, as I was still playing in Richard's stead at night.

But my 'vacation' was drawing to an end, and when the month in Trouville was over I returned to Paris with my brother and his partner, although I knew it could not be for long.

Dick had an engagement at the Cirque d'Eté and now fortunately was able to resume his act. All I had to do, therefore, was to wait until I heard from Mr. Lauri telling me when and where to join him. I doubt if I should remember anything especially about this period but for an acquaintance I made with a steeplechase jockey named Duff, a native of Ayrshire, with whom I became great pals.

Scottie Duff, as we called him, was a curious but extremely interesting character. He had had one or two bad falls in steeplechasing and I think had become extremely discouraged and pessimistic, and more or less lost heart in riding.

One afternoon I met him on one of the boulevards and he asked me if I had any money. Like most of us in those days, one day Scottie would be very well off and on another day dead broke.

As I was not working then, but had to depend on what my brother cared to give me for pocket money, naturally I couldn't help very much, so Scottie suggested that I should go along with him and see a "client" of his who was manager of a large café-restaurant by Porte St. Denis.

He rehearsed me on the way.

"Now, you're one of the head lads from Chantilly," he said. "You have brought some horses from there that are running at Maison Lafitte. One is a cert winner, but you won't tell me because I've nothing to give you... you see? So I've brought you along to see this gentleman... a client of mine... and if he cares to give me two louis there's one for you and one for me... and you let him know the name of the horse..."

"Well, what is the name of the horse?" I asked.

"Wait a minute," he said. "I hadn't thought of that. I'll pick one out of the paper."

He took a Paris "Sport" from his pocket glanced down the list of entries for the next day's racing, and said "Porte Veigne."

"Now," he added, "that's the name of the horse, and when I ask you the name in English, that's all you've got to say."

In due course we arrived at the Café-Restaurant, and as we entered an idea seemed to strike Scottie that I didn't quite fit the part. "Bend a little more," he said, "and walk bow-legged. If they look at you the way you really look, they'll know you've never been on a horse in your life." Which was pretty nearly true.

We sat at a little table in the café, and the manager came along, and Scottie at once began to tell his tale. In a short time the gentleman had produced his little leather purse and Scottie had his two louis.

Passing one to me he said, "Now, sonny, what is this dead cert?"

And when I mentioned Porte Veigne, the manager looked at Scottie and said, "But, Scottie, that's never been in the first three."

Said Scottie, "I know that. Look at the price it'll be."

The next day I looked up the results of the day's racing. There were only three runners in Porte Veigne's race – and he was third.

But Scottie had to make some money somehow, and whether he ever went back to that café or not I don't know. I didn't.

This was the same Scottie Duff who a few years later went to South Africa and eventually became a prominent trainer. I believe he died there, some few years ago.

At last came the expected letter from Charles Lauri. I was not to go back to England, after all, at least for some time, but was to join the company at Lille, where they were engaged to put on an old piece called "Round the World in Eighty Days," in which "The Sioux," which we had previously played as a separate sketch, was introduced as a scene.

The show was successful enough, but what I remember most keenly about that visit to Lille was my first introduction to the bull-fight, an experience which left me curiously both saddened and thrilled.

These bull-fighters (a second class lot, as I came to discover afterwards) had come over from Marseilles to hold a Sunday toro in the arena at Lille. During the week they had come in to the theatre and we had all become very well acquainted, with the perfectly natural result that the company arranged to go on the Sunday to the bull-fight in state, as guests of the toreadors.

So, when the day came, we all drove to the arena in open landaus, gaily adorned in the bull-fighters' sombreros. I was to play the part of the Mayor in the Box, who receives the cloaks as the bull-fighters march into the ring, and throws down the key to open the gate and release the bulls.

It was a gay and wonderful afternoon, but it very nearly ended in tragedy.

Charlie Lauri had perched himself on the edge of the arena with his camera, to get some snapshots of the "game." As the gate was opened he got himself all poised to take the picture and then, as the young bull came rushing towards where he previously sat, either his excitement or his enthusiasm got the better of him; he slipped, clutched at the top of the palisade on which he was perched, missed, and fell with a crash right into the ring.

Almost before he fell, the bull had seen him. Here was something to attack. Before Lauri could pick himself up the animal was rushing on him with death in its eyes, and only the presence of mind of one of the bull-fighters who deflected the mad rush with his cloak prevented what might have been a disaster.

But the incident was not without its happy side, for it served, at any rate, to put the spectators into a good temper, and they screamed with laughter. Which was all to the good, for it was not a particularly good show as bull-fights go and up to that time they had been none too pleased with the prospects of the entertainment.

Years later I saw a far more important bull-fight at Bordeaux. The first bull I saw killed disgusted me and turned me inside out, so that I was violently sick, but after

I had seen three bulls butchered I had to admire the amazing courage of these little men against the bull, for it seemed to me that it was then either man or bull.

The killings did not seem to me so very brutal then, but really I would have liked to see the act take place earlier in the fight. The real cruelty, it seems to me, is in the torment which the animal has to suffer before it is actually put to death; but this is only an after-conclusion, for so exhilarating and thrilling is the spectacle of the fight, and so carried away is the spectator by the excitement and shouting of the crowd whenever the toreador makes a clever move that he loses sight of the cruelty and finds himself shouting and cheering with the rest.

But it is a cruel sport, and I do not like it.

After Lille we went back to London, this time to the Canterbury Music Hall, where Lauri produced a new sketch called "The Housewarming," our leading lady in this being the wife of the late Fred Storey.

Very often during rehearsals she would bring her little baby girl with her and sometimes I would nurse the little mite while her mother was rehearsing. That little girl is now the Countess Poulett, mother of the young Earl who was recently married.

A short run in London, and we took "The Housewarming" to Paris, and played it in French at the Parisiana Theatre, two or three of the principal parts being played by French artistes.

On the same bill was Harry Potts, known to the world as Harry Fragson. It was my first meeting with Fragson, but we took to each other instinctively and many happy times since then have we spent in each other's company. Even at this time we made a cheery occasion of it "seeing Paris" together.

After a run of about eight weeks with "The Housewarming" in Paris we returned once more to London, where we played various sketches, filling in the weeks in London and the provinces until the pantomime season came round again.

Now came a series of years at the Lyceum and on Boxing Day in 1893 we opened in Oscar Barrett's production of "Santa Claus."

This show was, I believe, the first time pantomime was played with an interval. Hitherto, productions of this sort had been continuous, and the audience was expected to sit steadily and uninterruptedly through from beginning to end, three hours and a half or more. From the moment the curtain rang up, perhaps at 7.30 until quite possibly 11.30 the poor audience must stay where it was or miss a part of the show.

Obvious as this seems now, it was Oscar Barrett who first put into practice the simple but very sensible plan of breaking off for a quarter of an hour in the middle of the show to give the audience a chance to stretch their legs or take a drink or talk about the show.

For this "Santa Claus" production we played matinees only, for Sir Henry Irving was playing nights at the Lyceum throughout the season.

Often I used to meet the great man, and this was the first time I had met either Irving or Ellen Terry in person, though I had seen them on the stage many times. My father had known him well, for indeed many years before this, Irving had played comic swell to my father's clown at the Queen's Theatre, Manchester.

Henry Irving was then playing small parts in a stock company and in those old days it was the custom for a few members of a stock company to be kept on for pantomime, but only if they could dance. Consequently, some five or six weeks before pantomime season was due, it was no uncommon sight to see them all down at the theatre in the early morning putting in dancing practice and hoping to catch the eye of the proprietor.

And thus it was that at Manchester Irving was taken on for the Harlequinade in which he played comic swell for the splendid remuneration of thirty-five shillings a week!

There was a sort of sequel to this many years later when I went to a matinee at the Alhambra, Bradford, to see H. B. Irving playing his father's part Sergeant Brewster in "A Story of Waterloo."

Hearing I was in the theatre, he very courteously sent his manager round and invited me to his dressing room, where we had a pleasant chat and I mentioned this fact of his father having played with my own father in the Harlequinade.

H. B. said he had often heard Sir Henry himself mention this and described how he used to laugh when he spoke of his entrance and how his tall hat would be knocked off by "the funny clown."

Fine people these Irvings were. I have nothing but admiration for them. Sir Henry's kindnesses indeed are a byword, but very few people really realise how much good he did and "blushed to find it fame." Not so long ago, indeed, I had a reminder of this when, after the death of my old friend Harry Paulo, in going through some papers of his, those of his friends who tried to straighten out his affairs discovered among piles of old correspondence several letters from Sir Henry Irving, each one of which had obviously enclosed a gift of money.

One of these letters I have now in which in the simplest way the great tragedian sends to the old clown "£3. 3s as a donation to your Benefit with every good wish." And that three guineas was obviously sent direct to Paulo so that the donor's name should not be broadcast in any official list of donations.

I remember, too, not so long ago, the death of an old actor in a mean street in Islington. No relatives could be traced, but among letters he left behind were again several from Irving each enclosing a guinea or two guineas just to help the old man along.

Actors are not so bad.

Chapter VI

This year of grace 1894 – when once pantomime was over – was very much a repetition of the year before – sometimes playing on the Continent, sometimes in London, sometimes in the English provinces, but always gaining experience and looking forward to the now regular pantomime season at the end of the year.

Again we went to the Lyceum, this time in Oscar Barrett's "Cinderella," with Ellaline Terriss as the loveliest Cinderella of the season, or any other season, and it was here I first met Gracie Lane, then playing a small part, but playing it so well that Barrett selected her for principal girl the following year.

After this pantomime our first engagement was at the South London Music Hall where we played "The Sioux" for six weeks.

At this time Mrs. Poole was the proprietress of the South London, and there was a long bar running the length of the entire side of the stalls, so that if you were of the thirsty kind, you could stand at the bar and watch the whole performance, and not suffer from thirst at all! At this time, too, there was still a chairman who announced the turns as they appeared.

When I was there the chairman was a man named Bob Courtney and naturally it was regarded as something of a privilege by the young bloods of the day to be allowed to sit at the chairman's table and ply him with drinks, cigars, and conversation. Bob Courtney's favourite drink I remember well; it was whisky hot, with lemon and sugar, and this used to be served with the sort of glass "crusher" that one rarely sees nowadays.

But he had to be pretty snappy at his job, for, should he be the least bit slack in announcing a turn, immediately there would be an outcry from the gallery boys of BOB-BOB-BOB-BOB... like a continuous catcall.

Most of the gentlemen of the sporting world of the day were regular visitors. Mr. Blacklock, for instance, patron of the famous scullers and proprietor of Bradshaw's Guide, and, among the boxing fraternity such folk as Ted Pritchard, Alf Suffolk, and Sam Blacklock. I should think that quite as much money was taken in those days at the bars of the "old South" as ever was received for admission.

And so on, music hall after music hall. In these early years my brother and I were wandering from place to place as Lauri made the dates. Shortly after South London, for example, we were in Marseilles again, and during this particular visit there occurred something which might easily have had a bearing on the whole future of the English music hall stage.

It was the one time when Charles Lauri and the British public saw fit to differ.

Lauri had arranged with the author of a play called "La Flamenca" for its production in London.

In this play there was to be a real production of a bull-fight, with the arena on the stage and real bulls and bull-fighters. The members of the troupe, including my brother and myself were also to play bull-fighters. Lauri had engaged several real toreadors who were then in Marseilles and also a very excellent pantomimist named Phillippe, and we were all instructed to grow those small pigtails which bullfighters affect.

So we all visited the barber and had our hair cut to the necessary style; that is, short all over except for a tuft on the crown of the head which is trained into a little tail.

On our return to London we were all measured for the costumes similar to those worn by the toreadors and matadors one sees in the streets of Seville – tight-fitting trousers, a short jacket something like a pea-jacket, vest cut low like the vest of an evening suit, double collars about an inch deep and a very narrow, ribbon-like black, blue or red tie; and finally, the broad-brimmed, flat-crowned, picturesque sombrero, and block-fronted, high-heeled shoes to finish off the costume.

And strict instructions from Lauri not to speak English in the streets, but to strive to pick up as much Spanish talk and chatter as we could from the bull-fighters!

No sooner, however, was this novel show announced in London than the trouble began.

"What! Bull-fighting in England!" said half the public.

"Wonderful idea! We'll see some real sport at last," said the other half.

Anyway, the fight was on, and although it had been arranged and widely published that no sharp instruments should be stuck into the bull at all – not even the little pointed arrows that are half the excitement of a bull-fight (these were replaced by a special little device which would only grip the skin), nothing could persuade the authorities to permit it – and so the "certainly not" party won the day, and "La Flamenca" was never produced this side of the Channel.

Which was hard luck on Lauri, for he had spent a good deal of money on it.

Although I've often wondered what sort of reception my brother Harry and I would have received when we went home to Lambeth garbed like a couple of Spaniards, with pig-tails that wouldn't wash off, I'm sure it would have been instructive.

Seriously, however, it was a tremendous disappointment for Lauri, whose greatest interest was in animals and their presentation to the public. And the absurdity of it was that Lauri was one of the most kind-hearted people to animals I have ever known. He loved them. In his time he was the greatest animal impersonator on the stage. Well I remember his wonderful impersonation of Sally, the famous chimpanzee at the Zoo which could count up to nine.

To perfect this performance he had studied Sally with amazing patience and persistence. On Sundays he would be seen in Sally's cage at the Zoo, making friends and watching her every movement. She permitted him to make a mask of her face, and when he was wearing this mask on the stage he was Sally to the life. I doubt if so perfect an impersonation of an animal has ever been done elsewhere.

But there was no bull-fight, and as the year drew to a close, again the Lauri troupe prepared for pantomime at the Lyceum for the third and, in my own case, the last time (for it was many, many years before I played in that famous old theatre again).

It was during the last week of this pantomime, "Robinson Crusoe," at the Lyceum that an incident happened which severed my connection with Charles Lauri.

One of the scenes in the harlequinade was a scene he had taken from "Le Voyage en Suisse," and in this there occurred some rather important trap work, in which the appropriate traps had to be opened and closed at a certain time – to the second.

The scene was just approaching this tricky moment when I saw that Harry Ewins, who should have done this bit of business with Lauri, was not there to pick up his cue. So, in the emergency and to prevent a wait, I stepped in, but unfortunately, not having rehearsed this myself, instead of turning Lauri to the left to throw him from the carriage (which was part of the scene) as I should have done, I turned him to the right and, I must admit, it spoiled his act.

Lauri lost his temper and used language to me which so annoyed me that I walked off the stage then and there, went to the dressing-room, changed my clothes and left the theatre.

That was my last appearance with Charles Lauri.

* * * * *

I was twenty-one when I parted from him after six years of real, full-time stage experience that had given me confidence and developed what latent abilities I possessed.

It was a serious break. From that moment I might have become anything. I was lost, but, as I see now that was perfectly natural. I frequented the place which pros frequent, and a week or two later, happening to meet in the Canterbury Lounge a man whom I had known for some time and whose name was Charles Cardon, something like the following conversation ensued:

"Hello, Charlie, how's things?"

"'Hm. Hello, Fred! Not so bad; how's things with you?"

"'Mm. I've just left Lauri."

"Oh, yes?" (Show of interest) "I've just left my partner. (He had, as I knew, been working sketches with a partner called Ovid.) What about joining up?"

And that was the beginning of a new partnership. We agreed to work together playing sketches or any other darn thing we could do.

It wasn't any walkover, but we managed to fix a contract within a week or two at the Britannia, Glasgow, at £7. 10s for the week between us, and pay our own fares.

We still had a week after fixing the contract to get there, but we were worried. For, how were we to find the fares? There was nowhere we could borrow it, for it was winter – and I have to say that my mother was enough the "pro" never to have any money in the winter season!

However, I was lucky enough to snap up a week in a comedy sketch at the Albert Music Hall, Canning Town, and got just enough out of it to pay our expenses to Glasgow – by boat from St. Catherines Dock to Grangemouth.

But we opened on the Monday night in a very nervous state. And so would you have done if you had the same experience as we had had when we turned up on the Monday morning to rehearsal.

The stage manager was a genuine product of the Clyde, and when he saw us he demanded, "What's yer-r business? Ar-re ye funny?"

We told him we were dramatic sketch artistes. His whole body exuded disapproval.

"Then ye'll no' be ony guid here," he replied. "They' no' hae ye. D'ye no' ken the Britannia audience?"

I explained to him that it was our first visit to the city, and he cheered us up by saying, "Then ye'll get the burr-rrd."

But in spite of that we did go on. The audience were very quiet all the way through our show, but our sketch had to finish with a very realistic knife fight and that got them a bit worked up, which encouraged us so much that we began really to put our hearts into it, and were soon fighting almost in real earnest. In the excitement, in fact, my partner put the knife right through my right hand, and by the time they rang down the curtain we were both covered with blood.

They loved it.

And so successful was it that, in spite of the fact that I carry the scar on my hand to this day, we did get the Livermore tour and went triumphantly on to Aberdeen, Dundee and Newcastle.

It was at Aberdeen that a rather comic difference arose between us and our landlady. We found a bar kept by a man called, I think, Stevens or Stevenson, a man with a very good name for befriending members of the profession. One morning, while sitting in the snug little parlour of the house with my partner, a rough-looking fellow came in with something bulging under his coat. He got into conversation with us and eventually produced a salmon weighing about twelve pounds.

He asked us if we would buy it for four shillings, but though it looked good to us, we could only muster three. We got is finally at our price.

With visions of a much-wanted delightful supper we carried the fish to the digs and asked the landlady to cook half of it for that night's meal and keep the rest to make fish cakes and such like for dinner and supper the next day. In fact, I believe we had worked it out to last a whole week.

The woman's face was a study.

"Tak' it oot o' the hoose," she screamed. "I'll no' ha'e it aboot the place. D'ye no' ken I'm under a penalty?"

Cockneys that we were we didna ken, until she explained that the salmon had undoubtedly been poached, and was also out of season. With heavy hearts we took it down to the theatre at night, cut up into four pieces, and sold the pieces at a shilling each, so that although we missed a wonderful meal, at least we made a profit, and what the other performers on the bill said to their landladies was no concern of ours!

Although we seemed to have started so well, dates certainly did not come in anything like fast enough to keep our initial success and after about five weeks we were back in London again – dateless. Cardon joined Brooke and Mortimer, sketch artistes, as a comedian, and that put an end to our short-lived partnership.

Chapter VII

At this time my mother and father were living in a small house in Paris Street, facing St. Thomas's Hospital, and my brother-in-law, J.P. Sutherland, and my sister were staying with us.

This was lucky for me, because J.P. had a two weeks' engagement to fill at the old theatre in Gravesend – the Grand, I believe it was called – and the first week was playing Dion Boucicault's "The Octoroon." He engaged me to play Wan-ha-Teh, the Indian.

The second week we played "Donnybrook" and my brother-in-law, who was rather too fond of having substantial "subs" from the management, would, I am afraid, have been unable to pay us at the end of the week had it not been for a young gentleman turning up and putting down £60 as a premium so that he might learn acting-management.

That young man was Walter Stephenson who, until a few months ago, was acting manager at the Palace, Halifax.

Walter Stephenson and I became life-long friends, and the time came when we shared a good many hardships together as well as a good many successes.

From Gravesend we went to Chatham and played two weeks, and then had two weeks out, and things began to look not too good once more.

And right there friend Stephenson had his first taste of the trials of an acting manager.

Sutherland fixed a fortnight at the Haymarket Theatre, Liverpool, then under the management of Fred Wilmott, whom I remembered some time before this as an Irish comedian working with a partner as Farrell and Wilmott.

But how to get to Liverpool? A fortnight wasted in Chatham had depleted Sutherland's meagre resources until they were in fact nil. However, by dint of scraping among us all we raised enough for the bare fare, but were unable to pay our diggings, so poor Stephenson – this budding new acting-manager who had put £60 in real money to learn all about it – was left behind in pawn for our bills until J.P. could send back the money from Liverpool to redeem him and the private luggage!

The second week at Liverpool, Sutherland booked up Tom McInerny, a Liverpool wrestler, and several other wrestlers, and a contest was put into the bill, members of the audience being invited to come up to the stage and wrestle with these local stars. Of course this was all faked, and the contestants from the audience who were accepted for battle were all on the pay-roll.

To me wrestlers had always seemed a bit out of place on a music hall stage, and my opinion on this matter got rude confirmation that Saturday night when I went into my brother-in-law's room to draw my salary.

Three or four of our wrestling gentlemen were there before me – and there seemed to be some little difference –

for the best wrestling contest of the week was going on. So I decided I would leave the little matter of my pay just then.

And it would have been all the same, anyway, for it was an unlucky week – and Walter Stephenson and I found ourselves left high and dry on the rocks there in Liverpool.

The next few days we spent hanging about the town, haunting the theatres and the hotels and hoping for the best. Sometimes we would go into the Bee Hotel, a well-known theatrical house of its day, kept by a gentleman named Tom Bush.

One day I noticed a stranger talking to Mr. Bush and they both kept looking over to the corner where Walter and I sat, trying to make a cup of coffee last as long as possible. Finally Bush called me over and introduced me to the stranger, who said he wanted a man to open next Monday in a drama called "The Career of Crime" and to play an old gentleman in the first act and the light comedy role in the later part of the play.

I accepted the engagement and signed the contract there and then – a contract written on half-sheets of cream-laid hotel notepaper – and my friend Stephenson also fixed himself up as acting manager and to play a small part in the second act.

We were to rehearse the remainder of the week and open on the following Monday at the Theatre Royal, Garston.

When we arrived at Garston we were introduced to the proprietor who, by the way, was Dave Barnard, who at one time had the Falstaff in Old Street, London. This was then a public house with a kind of a music hall at the back and I may mention that many famous stars appeared there in their earlier days.

In due course came Monday night, and we opened. In the first act I played a sort of Mr. Bullion, a rich and elderly City banker, but I've often wondered whether in spite of grey wig and side-whiskers anybody in the audience was deceived into thinking I fitted the part; so I was always glad when the last scene of the first act came round and I was strangled by the villain and allowed to change into the light comedy rôle.

We received our money that Saturday night, returned to Liverpool, paid up the landlady, and on the Sunday travelled to Middleton.

At the time I am speaking of, the theatre at Middleton was a wooden building, and two large coke fires stood in the stalls. These were enough to dope the audience, let alone the additional soporific effects of our dismal drama. But in spite of it we played the week, only, I am sorry to say that on this Saturday night once more the Ghost did not walk.

Most of us, I suppose, were able to give our landladies a few shillings. At least, Walter and I did, and then the members of the "Career of Crime" company held a meeting and sacked the proprietor for bringing a company on the road without the money to back it up. And as the play was the property of one of the members of the cast we took matters into our own hands.

We heard that Heywood, a small place some few miles away, was vacant, and somehow we raked up together enough to send the ladies of the company on by train – the married couples going together – and Walter

Stephenson, Mowbray Harle and myself walked at the side of the cart that carried our props.

After seeing everyone else fixed up in digs of some sort, Walter and I searched around for a place where we could stay that night. We asked a policeman if he knew where we could put up and where it would not cost too much, and he directed to a large, forbidding sort of house just outside the town and standing with rather a dilapidated air on a large piece of what looked like waste ground.

We could find no knocker or bell, so we tapped on the door and a voice called from within, "Coom in."

We pushed the door open then and found ourselves in a big kitchen, with paving-stone floor and a huge fireplace. Seated at a table in the centre of the room were an elderly man and a woman and a young girl – apparently their daughter.

As we entered the girl remarked, "Eh, it's actor chaps." We enquired whether we could have a room for the night, and the man in broad Yorkshire asked, "D'yeh want private room?"

When we said we did he replied, "Well, coom this way. Put names in book." So we signed a book stating where we had come from and he said, "That'll be foorpence each."

Then we understood. We were in a fourpenny doss house!

The man took a small piece of candle and lit us up some stone stairs. We walked through a room with five or six beds on either side, all occupied – and the place smelled like it!

At the end of the room was a matchwood partition with a door, and behind this in a corner a small iron bedstead scarcely large enough to hold one. This was the private room. Anyway, we managed to squeeze in and lay there back to back uncomfortable until the morning.

Then we went out and met the rest of the company and Stephenson had a talk with the manager of the little local theatre, the Reform Club. We arranged to open on the Thursday night, playing Thursday, Friday and Saturday.

A local printer did us a few bills and we had about fifty big lithographs of a play called "The Lights o' London" that was or had been running in London. (I've no idea how those bills got into the possession of the "Career of Crime," but it doesn't matter now!) The picture, I remember, was of a woman fainting in the snow, with a policeman shining his bulls-eye torch down on to her and a sympathetic crowd gathered round.

It had nothing whatever to do with our own play, "The Career of Crime," nor did it resemble any scene in it, however one might stretch one's imagination – but they were the only large bills we had, and they had to go up!

We billed the town and Stephenson and myself put on frock coats and tall hats (out of the props basket) and worked the bills at dinner time, handing out the small bills to the girls as they poured out of the gates – and had rather a jolly time doing it, too!

The result was that we opened to a pretty good house on the Thursday and people seemed to enjoy the show. Then, the next day, I set out for Radcliffe – on foot – to try and arrange for the following week.

I dare say a good deal has been written elsewhere of the old days of the "dry-ups" – those unfortunate companies which set out on tour without sufficient financial backing, and after running two or three weeks come to a dead-end when, if mother won't send the fare, you have nothing to do but pad the hoof for home (boots permitting).

But no book of this kind would really be complete without some reference to them, and indeed my own experiences were now making me all too painfully familiar with this side of the profession.

* * * * *

My journey from Heywood to Radcliffe on the Friday morning after our mid-week opening was one of sheer optimism, for I knew about what possibilities there might be of getting a theatre.

Finally, however, I discovered that the building was under the control of a local solicitor. I found him, and we came to terms. For £2 a night, he said, we might have the theatre, but he would want £2 deposit to start with. So, hoping that Heywood was still going strong, I promised him he should have the £2 the following day and we would open on the Monday.

Then I got into touch with a printer in the town and got him to run off two hundred day-bills. Then I went back to Heywood, where we were delighted to find that once more we had a fairly good house; indeed, for us, a very good house, and we really began to feel that we might see it through, after all.

Next morning Stephenson and I went round the shops and pubs and collected again our "Lights o' London" posters which had been shown in the shop windows, or were not too much damaged for further use. Although I must say that even the best of them were now a long way from perfect for they had all done duty a good many times, sometimes stuck to the walls with stamp-edging, sometimes scorched by the sun in a window, and in any case handled and folded by many hands. But shabby and dilapidated though they were we did not propose to lose them.

And on Sunday the "Career of Crime" Company left for Radcliffe. It was not a very long journey, but we had to change on the way, and, when we had changed, to our horror we discovered that our valuable "Lights o' London" posters were not on the train!

The station-master was called, a great fuss was made, and we had the poor fellow telephoning all along the line in the hope of tracing those missing lithographs – but all to no avail. Most incensed of all, however, was Stephen Vast, our 'heavy' man, who threatened the railway company with the direst penalties including the Spanish Inquisition if they were not found; and it suddenly dawned on Stephenson and me why he took the loss of those shabby old bills so much to heart.

Whomever did the "billing" had naturally to visit all the local hostelries, and this is the way we imagined that it was done by Stephen Vast, on whom this duty usually fell.

Entering a hotel or public-house he would respectfully ask permission to "display one or two of these bills in your window, sir," and then would add grandiloquently, "and of course, sir, if you would like to see the show on the Friday night, we should be delighted to welcome you."

Sometimes the reply might run, "Nay, lad, Ah've seen enough rubbish at yon theayter," but in other cases the publican would more or less graciously accept a pass.

Then Stephen would go through the careful ceremony of writing out the pass for one. The landlord could then be relied on to say something to the effect that,

"Eh, lad, that's nae good to me, thee knowst; I'll have to take missus along wi' me, too," which was Stephen's cue for taking back the single pass and ceremoniously writing out another to admit two.

Which in nine cases out of ten would mean a free drink with the landlord. No wonder Stephen Vast wanted to find those "Lights o' London" bills. But they never turned up, in spite of our threats to the stationmaster.

However, this was only the first of our troubles. We arrived at Radcliffe and found ourselves digs. Then in the evening Walter Stephenson and I strolled round the town taking stock of our chances.

During our stroll we called in at The Boar's Head, and here we made friends with one of the landlord's sons, a youth named Tom Aldred. He turned out to be a very good fellow and after we had talked a while he made us up half a pail of paste, and lent us a whitewashing brush and a Windsor chair (to serve as "steps"), and after closing time, and sheltered by the darkness of the night, Tom Aldred, Stephenson and myself set out to bill the town with two hundred day-bills I had ordered two days earlier.

Some of these bills were posted where bills have never been posted before – on the railings of private houses, on private hoardings, on barns, or anywhere we could find a vacant spot, and the good people of Radcliffe awoke the next morning to find themselves surrounded by "The Career of Crime."

The following morning Walter and I swept out the hall, dusted the seats, and generally cleaned up the place, for we had found it in a shocking state. Then we called on my old friend the Solicitor and paid the £2 deposit for the theatre.

Then out of the prop basket again came those tall hats and frock coats, and once more we posted ourselves at the mill gates at dinner time and distributed handbills to all the lads and lassies of the town.

Evening came, and off to the theatre we went, ready to paralyse the inhabitants with that sensational drama (as played in London) "The Career of Crime." But judge of our astonishment and horror when, on arriving there, we found a sergeant and two police-constables waiting for us at the doors. At once Stephenson and I jumped to the conclusion that we had overstepped all the marks with our fly-posting, and that we were for it!

But no. It was worse than that. The sergeant told us that the licence of the theatre had run out – and no play could be given in it!

So round we rushed to our solicitor, who luckily lived over his office. He said he was awfully sorry, but he had forgotten to renew the licence, and that was that. Nothing could be done about it now. We couldn't open. But we could have our £2 deposit back if we liked!

We took it back.

And that, as far as I ever heard, was the end of "The Career of Crime." It had been a career of misfortune. One by one the members of the company got small engagements here and there, or went back home, or just drifted away.

But four of us found ourselves a little group of castaways – Walter Stephenson, Mowbray Harle, a man named Frank Crellin, and myself. The question was, what were we to do? We talked over all sorts of plans – starting new companies, forming a comedy team, and all kinds of fantastic ideas, and, all the while, the few shillings we had left were dwindling away and away....

Before long it got to a point where we had to earn our meals or go without, and it was then that I remembered our kind friend of the "Boar's Head," young Tom Aldred. So down to the "Boar's Head" I went, and asked permission to do a song or two or a recitation to entertain the company in the smoke room.

This they let me do, and it was so successful that Tom paid me two shillings for writing out a copy of the recitation I had given, and then himself passed the hat round and collected the comparatively handsome total of about five shillings.

So we were in funds again and I went along and told the good news to my three companions in distress and we all went back to the "Boar's Head," where this time we went into the "back parlour" and gave a joint show to the miners who used the place. Between us we kept up the entertainment for a couple of hours and in return the company kept us regaled with tripe on skewers and mugs of ale.

For a week this was our sole means of livelihood, but then we had a stroke of luck; at least, Stephenson did, for his brother Albert generously sent him £5, which Walter equally generously used to pay up the diggings for all of us for another week and then, after buying himself a ticket home to Birmingham, divided between us what he had left.

After a sad farewell Stephenson left and it was some years before we ever happened to work together again, although we kept in touch always.

The night before he went, the miners had one of their regular "do's" – a big hot supper at the "Boar's Head" –

and we were invited to the feast as entertainers. The long white tables in the pleasant, old-fashioned bar-parlour simply groaned under the weight of food and spiced ale in tremendous jugs, and by about nine o'clock everyone was in a delightfully happy state.

Just about this time an argument arose about wrestling, and friend Stephenson, who rather prided himself on being a bit of a wrestler, and myself, who felt that I had seen enough to know something about it, joined in. The upshot of it was that Walter and I volunteered to give our hosts an exhibition bout. After all, we were there to entertain them, and we stripped to the waist, and set to, amid the cheers of the audience.

But I was unlucky; hardly had we got started when Walter threw me, my fist struck the end of a loose plank in the floor, the other end of the plank came up and hit me right between the eyes, and I was out! When, about three quarters of an hour later, I recovered consciousness I decided that wrestling was definitely not for me. For days I carried about with me two black eyes and a severe sick headache. No; I was certainly not destined to be a wrestler.

Anyway, Stephenson left, and then there were three.

A day or two later Mowbray Harle managed to get enough money to pay his fare to Glasgow, and then there were two.

Years later I played at the Empire at Glasgow, and Harle was then manager there. It takes a lot to get an old pro down!

But Crellin and I, left behind, were at the end of our resources and even bar parlour entertaining could not provide us with a living for ever. We could not find a copy of "The Stage" in the town, and as this was the only medium we knew likely to help us to find work we decided to walk to Manchester to look at a copy.

So we set off on foot to Manchester. Already in Radcliffe I had pawned my only pawnable possession – a silver watch – for ten shillings, and before we started for Manchester I called on the pawnbroker and asked if he could give me a little more on it. Rather out of goodness of heart, I think, than good business, he advanced me another two shillings, which, after deducting the cost of the ticket, left us 1s 11¼d and this was our total capital.

In due course we got to Manchester, where the first man I met was Gus Hammond, later to become my own manager, who had been stage manager with Oscar Barrett when I played in pantomime at the Crystal Palace.

"Well, well," he said. "Fancy seeing you. How are you doing?"

"Oh, splendidly, old chap; splendidly," I replied.

Then he asked us to have a drink, but, gasping as we were, we declined, for the old pro wise in his generation is careful to whom he reveals the fact when he's down....

But all the same, Crellin and I made for Cox's Bar, and happily it was "free lunch" time and the hot-pot was on. We had two glasses of bitter and the barmaid handed us a small plate each of hot-pot and a piece of bread. I don't know whether she noticed how quickly it disappeared, but she enquired if we would like a little more. We feared it "wasn't done" so we refused, but we both felt that we could have eaten the entire hot-pot, saucepan and all.

We looked through the "wanted" column of The Stage which we found in the bar, but the only local engagement we could find was one for two character actors at Middleton, the town of not-very-pleasant memories.

Back then we walked to Radcliffe, and arrived there about two hours before the "Boar's Head" was due to close, dead tired and with feet sore from our day's walk of twenty-two miles or so. But for all that we managed once more to put in a little entertaining in the friendly bar of the "Boar's Head," getting some beer and tripe for our supper and a few shillings which the kindly miners and others collected for us.

What good pals these miners were. Rough and uncouth they may have been, but they were very human and very kind of heart. I think they really regretted that we were leaving them and when we parted the handshakes and the good wishes they gave us were hearty and sincere. And, too, were those of the genial landlord, Mr. Aldred, and his three sons, George, Tom, and a younger brother who was killed a little later in a pit accident.

Next morning we were up early and after settling up with the landlady we were about 10d strong, but, nothing daunted, and like Mazeppa again we "urged on our wild career," and set out to walk from Radcliffe to Middleton.

There we found the proprietress of the company, a Miss Emily Burke, who informed us that she was the niece of the great Scottish tragedian, Henry Talbot, and that she was then running a repertory. The following week they were going to Ilkley for three nights and Otley for the other three, and if we liked to join them we could do so at £3 joint per week for the tour.

We accepted readily and were invited to watch the show that evening from the front, so once again we made the acquaintance of the old Theatre Royal, where we sat among the coke fumes and watched our new friends on the stage.

After the last act we went round behind and I knocked at the door of Miss Burke's dressing room, really to ask for a little money in advance, but before I could speak she said, "Oh, I know what you've come for," and going back into the dressing room handed me half a dozen manuscripts.

"Here you are," she explained. "On Monday night we play 'Hamlet.' Mr. Crellin will play the King of Denmark and Polonius, and you, Mr. Kitchen, will play the Ghost and double the King."

I was flabbergasted! "Hamlet!" And up to that moment I doubt if I had seen a Shakespearean play on the stage, let along played in one.

"On Tuesday," she went on, regardless of my astonishment, "we play 'The Private Secretary.' Mr. Crellin will play the Rev. Robert Spalding and you Mr. Cattermole. On Wednesday we play 'The Shaughraun.' Mr. Crellin will play Con and you Corrie Kinchleah. Will you kindly copy your parts out from the script."

And this was Saturday night, and we had to open on the Monday! But had she thrown "Macbeth," "The School for Scandal" and "The Belle of New York" into the bargain, I should still have made the same reply, "Yes, that'll be quite all right, madam."

But all the same I was so astounded that I almost forgot the important errand that had taken me to the dressing room, and it was only when Crellin gave me a nudge that I remembered to stammer, "Er – would it be convenient for us to have a little sub?"

"Oh, certainly," she replied, much to our satisfaction, "Would you mind waiting in the passage a moment?"

We waited several minutes, then the door opened, she quickly pressed three coins into my hand, and wished us a good night with the air of a queen of tragedy that she was. We made our way hurriedly through the dark passage and out into the street again, I clutching my Gladstone bag and the manuscripts and Crellin his brown-paper parcel – the only luggage we possessed. We dashed into the nearest pub, ordered two glasses of beer, and then at last I opened my right hand, expecting to see therein the welcome glitter of three golden sovereigns; but all that we do see is the disappointing dullness of three shillings – the old lady's idea of what we required to carry us on. And we had had no food that day!

So we swallowed our beer and our disappointment and went out into the night again to try to find some lodgings, but whether it was our appearance as "actor chaps" or that the local landladies remembered too well the "Career of Crime" I cannot say, but we could get no lodgings.

By half past eleven we were so desperate that we went into the local police station and asked permission to sleep in a cell.

The inspector considered the matter for a moment and then said, "No, I'm afraid I couldn't do that." We told him we could find no other shelter whatever and should have to walk about all night.

"Sorry," he said, "but I can't let you stay here. But I'll drop a hint to the boys going on night duty not to interfere if they come across you anywhere."

It was drizzling with November rain as we began to tramp about again. Our steps turned back towards the theatre and near this we came across a building with a somewhat sheltered portico, with three steps leading up to a padlocked door.

At least it would keep the rain off us, and with a sigh of relief I sat down on the top step and huddled into the corner, leaning against the door-post. Then I dropped off to sleep, but somewhere about four o'clock in the morning I woke up, shivering with cold and so stiff that I could hardly move.

In the dim light of a street lamp I saw Frank Crellin standing, the script of "Hamlet" in his hand, reading up the parts of the King and Polonius. Fortunately for Frank, being a graduate of Cambridge, he was fairly familiar with his Shakespeare, but still he had to learn the parts, and when better than in the quiet of the early morning hours in a deserted street?

When he saw that I was awake, he came over to the doorstep and did his best to inspire me with the spirit of my own part. Perhaps you can imagine my feelings – a pantomimist, sitting on a doorstep, cold, stiff and very hungry – and discussing how the ghost of Hamlet's father should be played!

Chapter VIII

That ordeal at Middleton stands out in my memory even today as typical of the hardships that many a mummer, destined perhaps to success and fame in the future, or perhaps fated never to rise above the rank and file of our profession, has had to undergo. I will say frankly that to me, while it lasted, it was a nightmare.

Years afterwards, when I had managed to climb a good deal higher up the ladder of success, and these days seemed so remote that one could hardly believe they ever existed, I drove over from Manchester in my car to see Middleton again and because perhaps it had been the scene of so trying a moment in my life, because perhaps we are all at heart sentimental – certainly I am, I wanted to show my wife that doorstep on which I had spent so unpleasant, if perhaps romantic, a night, I said to my wife on the way:

"I'd like to buy that doorstep."

"Very well," she said. "Do, if you like, only I suppose you'll have to buy the building with it."

"M'm. I suppose so. But that doesn't matter. It seemed like a pretty good building, and I suppose we could do something with it."

But, alas! for my sentimental plans. When we arrived, there was nothing there but a hoarding. The building had been demolished – and the doorstep had gone!

But on that dark morning it was there all right, and when, with the dawn, a milkman came clattering along the street we knew we had had enough of it, and decided that it was "time to get up." So we bought two pennyworth of milk each for our "breakfast" and took the milkman's brilliant suggestion that the railway station would be open by then and there might be a fire in the waiting room.

There was – it was just being lighted by a sleepy porter – and soon we were seated as comfortably as possible before it, the steam rising in clouds from our rain-soaked clothes. With our pocket handkerchiefs and some water from the station tap we brightened ourselves up as best we could, and soon the company began to arrive and Miss Burke introduced us to the different members.

Another novel little experience awaited me when the train came in. As we made for our seats Miss Burke asked me if I had my luggage, and when I pointed to my Gladstone bag she asked me if I would please put it in the guard's van. I noticed friend Crellin making odd grimaces, but didn't "get" him, and in due course put the bag in the van with the props and general baggage of the company.

When a few minutes later, I joined Crellin in our compartment, he said, "We've struck it again. Why did you put our bags in the guard's van?"

Still dense, I looked at him and asked, "What do you mean?"

"It's the old, old story," he said. "We're travelling on the baggage. When we arrive at Ilkley the stuff will not be released until the fares are paid."

I should have guessed it myself, for when we arrived we found that he was right, and our only consolation was that Miss Burke confidently assured us that "it would be all right on Monday morning."

As usual, we walked around the town looking for digs. This time, for a change, we were lucky. The landlady was charming and I discovered that she was a sister of the well-known performer of that time, Lieutenant Travis, the ventriloquist, whose son, Frank Calvert, had been at Dr. Herniman's school with me. The landlady indeed apologised because she had nothing cooked except the remains of a rabbit and some pickled pork they had had for dinner, but she would serve them up with a few potatoes. Not having seen anything so substantial for quite a long time, it was a veritable banquet to us and we enjoyed it thoroughly.

Then the reaction was beginning to set in, and I was still feeling the effects of my night of exposure on the doorstep and the privations of the previous few days. So poor Frank Crellin had to put me to bed between the blankets and, like Nicholas Nickleby and Smike, had to sit at my bedside while he struggled manfully to teach me my part for the Ghost scene I had to play the following night.

On Monday morning I was feeling shaky, but got along to eleven o'clock rehearsal. We began to rehearse. I got as far as, "Now, Hamlet,

"'Tis given out that, sleeping in mine orchard,
"A serpent stung me – " but could get no further.

Dear old Crellin tried to put it right for me, and assured Miss Burke that I would be all right at night. Back at the digs we had a good dinner and another good go at the Ghost. Eventually, however, I had to give it up as a bad job.

"Frank," I said, "I shall never know a word of it. What am I to do?"

"Don't worry, Fred," said my trusty friend. "When you walk on in the battlement scene, keep as near the wings as possible. I'll be as near you as I can at the side and read it from the book. You just make the motions and let the audience think you are really speaking the words."

The night arrived and we went to the show. If the British public had the same idea about Shakespeare as I had that night, there would certainly never have been any festival at Stratford-on-Avon!

The baskets had arrived with the costumes, hired from James Carr of Liverpool, a man I met once or twice as an actor-costumier. The costume for the Ghost was not what I would call perfect. There was no visor, but a wig and a long grey beard and a piece of green muslin to drape over the top, spangled tights, silver shoes, and a sort of chain-mail pullover to complete the outfit.

Personally, it struck me that it would have done better for Neptune in a Christmas pantomime, but it has to be the Ghost, and a short piece of broomstick with white and blue foolscap wrapped round it for the scroll completed this original make-up.

Waiting for my entrance in the front cloth and standing ready in the wings I was feeling very ill and worried when the humorous side of it all struck me.

Suddenly it flashed across my mind that could my dad or my brother or anyone else who knew me have been in the front to see my entrance as the Ghost in "Hamlet" and have known that it was really me, what would have been their feelings? Would they have laughed, or pitied me? The situation was so genuinely comic that I started to laugh inwardly, and I absolutely shook, and, as I walked majestically across the stage, the stately Ghost of Hamlet's poor murdered father, passing Horatio, whispered,

"Hush, hush, hush,
"Here comes the bogey man."

Which very nearly dried him up!

Then, in Scene IV came my great ordeal. And, as I feared, when I came to "A serpent stung me, "I dried up. But Crellin, true to his promise, was close behind me armed with script and candle, and, as I paused he took up speech in as nearly the same voice as he could make it, while I moved my lips as though the words were mine.

And then he dried up!

Or so I thought, for his voice, to my dismay, had ceased. Desperately, I fumbled for something to say and in the meantime muttered, "Oh, Hamlet, oh, list," which was near enough to the spirit of the scene to pass muster until with relief I heard a tense whisper behind me, "Anybody got a match?" and guessed what had happened.

In his enthusiasm to support me, Frank had blown out the candle with his breath and left himself in the dark, and until it was lighted again the poor Ghost must do the best be could with "List, oh list!"

However, good old British public. They stood for it and more. Miss Burke was playing Hamlet, and if you can imagine a Hamlet looking like Betsy Trotwood and complete with a black ringlet wig, no more need be said!

Even now, however, the night's entertainment was not over, for after the first act the manager of the theatre brought round a local gentleman who wanted to meet the "distinguished Shakespearean company." After the introductions had been effected he invited the company to take a little refreshment with him. There was only one answer to that, and, as there was no bar in the theatre, our new friend went back to his house and returned in a few minutes with champagne for the ladies and three bottles of Scotch whisky and a dozen bottles of soda for the men. We thought he was an angel from heaven!

From that moment we all felt better. The whisky was there in the men's dressing room and we were all free – and indeed pressed – to help ourselves. Particularly the second gravedigger, who dug his pick so deeply into one of the bottles that – well, it led to another spot of bother.

The dressing room, it happened, was underneath the stage, and the grave "trap" opened almost in the centre of the dressing room ceiling. Two large baskets were placed under the trap for the gravedigger to stand on during his scene with a pail of mould and a spade. Of course, by this time, it being now Act 5 and the whisky having circulated handsomely, we thought it very funny to shake the baskets beneath him. By this time the second gravedigger was fairly "speechless," so he must have looked more like a farmer feeding chickens than a gravedigger digging a grave.

Now, it is lucky for the first gravedigger that in this scene he can always get rid of the second gravedigger whenever he likes by taking a short cut to the line, "Go, get thee to Yaughan; fetch me a stoup of liquor."

So, the first gravedigger, seeing how it was with the second gravedigger, dismissed him with the magic words. Exit second gravedigger, very indignant, but unable to do anything about it.

I was standing at the side and thought it would be a good opportunity to try out in practice an old gag that I had often heard my father speak of, but had never seen worked. I said to the indignant actor, "Go back and tell him they want a penny on the can!"

And, to my amazement, he actually did it. Back to the stage he went and remarked to his fellow clown, "Hic – the l-landlord wants a penny on the – hic – can!"

At which the other actor, knocked right off his balance, lifted his spade threateningly and shouted, "Get out, you silly ass...." And then....

Well, I have seen a good many performances of "Hamlet" since then, but if the laughter which greeted this scene is any standard, I have never seen the play enjoyed by the audience quite so much!

Such, then, was my first experience in Shakespeare, and after playing in "The Private Secretary" the following night and "Trilby" (Miss Burke had changed her original plan for this night) on Wednesday, Crellin and I received the generous honorarium of 13s 6d each, out of which we had to move ourselves to the next town!

And so to Otley, where things were even worse. There we got lodgings with a blind landlady, whose business was making socks by machine, and when she offered to make a pair for Crellin and me, we accepted them with a good deal more pleasure than their mere value should have warranted. But times were indeed hard.

Otley was a wash-out, and Miss Burke decided to go to Rawtenstall, where we hoped things would improve. I remember the place for two reasons – one, because the theatre had the previous week been occupied by Professor Crocker's horses, and it smelt like it! And, two, because there we held a meeting of the company and decided to make it a commonwealth – a typical "dry-ups" arrangement.

Also that week, as the actor who had hitherto played Svengali in "Trilby" (in which the previous week I had played a minor part), left, I was cast for that important rôle.

Somehow I scrambled through it, and after the show, in accordance with our new commonwealth plan, came the share-out. My share came to three-halfpence!

The next day we were billed to play "Leah" – not "King Lear," but a then-popular drama about a Jewish maiden – and I was to play Jacob, but as the following week was still to be fixed it was arranged that I should go over to Runcorn and see Mr. Craddock, the proprietor of the theatre there.

We scraped together enough for my fare to Manchester and a few coppers to get me a sandwich on the journey. I arrived at Manchester, had a pork pie and a glass of beer and started to walk to my destination.

At Widnes I took a short cut by the side of a canal and came to a place where, to my dismay, I found that there was a penny toll-bridge leading into Runcorn – and I had not a penny left!

So there I was, stuck again, and almost within reach of my destination. Then I saw a large number of workmen – some hundreds of them – emerge from a nearby factory and I noticed that they were crossing the bridge without paying any toll. So my luck had held again; I pulled my cap down over my eyes, turned up the collar of my coat; looked as little like an actor as possible – and got across with the crowd. So I still owe somebody a penny.

I found my way to the theatre, ascertained Mr. Craddock's address, and went to his house. He invited me into a homely kitchen where the kettle was boiling on the hob, the cat sitting contentedly in front of a pleasant fire, and the master of the house enjoying an evening pipe. He told me his theatre was not booked up for the following week and I promised him we could play "Trilby" two nights, "The Private Secretary" two nights and "The Shaughraun" two nights.

He accepted the company and promised to arrange to pay our fares from Rawtenstall. I made out a day bill which I left for him to get printed.

Next problem was to get back to Rawtenstall. Would Mr. Craddock, I debated with myself, stand for a little loan – or should I be letting the company down? Anyway, I risked it; he readily advanced me half-a-crown, and so I was able to get back in comparative comfort to Rawtenstall, where I arrived just as the show was over. How on earth they got through the play with the tiny company that was left I still do not know.

I gave them my good news and went home to my digs, and there, for once, was some good news for me, for the landlady handed me a letter from London. It was a contract from Mr. Oscar Barrett for me to play Harlequin in the pantomime at Drury Lane, Mr. Barrett having taken over the panto on the sudden death of Sir Gus Harris.

And very luckily, too, for that week proved no better than other weeks had done, and, when Sunday came, once more we could not pay the landlady. But I showed her the Drury Lane contract and she permitted us to depart – subject to my leaving the old Gladstone bag behind again.

However, the company duly met at the station and then we discovered that Mr. Craddock had not carried out his promise and consequently the fares were not paid. So there ensued a long argument with the railway people, Miss Burke pleading and arguing and the stationmaster suspicious, but finally he let us go as far as Widnes, where we had that miserable toll-bridge to cross again – but at least we were able to manage.

On arriving at our destination Crellin and I obtained digs, and my first bit of luck was to break the water jug, which, of course, belonged to the landlady's great-great-grandmother, and which she would not have lost for thousands of pounds. She was very cross – until I showed her the Drury Lane contract!

We opened with "The Private Secretary," but either because we were all feeling horribly despondent or because the audience looked dangerously thin and utterly uninterested, the first act went very flat. Mr. Craddock, the proprietor, came round and said so, and put up a bright idea.

"Do you know any songs you could introduce?" he asked. "That might brighten the play up a bit. We can't have a flop the first night."

I agreed, but the only two songs I could think of which I knew well enough to put over were Alec Hurley's "I ain't a-goin' to tell" and Charlie Bignell's "More Work for the Undertaker."

I explained this to Mr. Craddock but I told him I had no music. However, as he and his wife were the band, violin and piano, he said that if I would hum over the tune they could vamp for me. The next problem was to introduce the songs into "The Private Secretary."

This is how I got out of it. I entered with Mr. Marsden and seating myself at table right began the following dialogue:

"You are very comfortable here, Marsden."
"Very comfortable indeed, Cattermole, old chap."
"But don't you long for the old bachelor days? What jolly times we used to have together."
"Do you remember those comic songs you used to sing, Cattermole?"
"I do indeed, Marsden."
"I wonder if you could remember them now?"
"I will try."

Cue for music.

This week my mother sent me a postal order to go home. We discovered that there was an excursion from Liverpool to London for Lord Mayor's Show Day, and it stopped at Runcorn. The train left something after midnight and the fare was about ten shillings. So we played that night and then with the ten shillings left out of my mother's remittance and a shilling or two we had received as our share, I was able to settle up with the landlady (including her precious water-jug) and give poor old Crellin 1s. 6d. He came to the station to see me off, and that was the last time I ever saw him. But I have never forgotten him and have always hoped that he, too, contrived ultimately to strike better times. I did hear from him once in Manchester, when he told me he had got a "shop," but he never wrote again, and so ended a pleasant friendship which was all the more sincere for the hard times we had shared.

The next morning, tired but happy to be back and to say good-bye, - at least for a time, - to the "Dry-ups," I arrived in London; and if my hair was rather long over my coat collar, and my possessions no longer enjoyed the dignity of my old Gladstone bag, and had instead to be carried in a somewhat disconsolate-looking brown paper parcel, I knew that all these things would soon be remedied, for did I not now possess that "Open Sesame" to all things, - the Drury Lane contract?

So, cheerfully I padded it home to Paris Street, and found my mother up and waiting for me with an excellent breakfast all hot and ready. It was Heaven again, and soon afterwards I was packed off to get a haircut, and then to the family tailors to get a new suit of clothes, so that I could go to rehearsal looking respectable, and not the down-and-out I had become.

Chapter IX

This pantomime, "Aladdin," at Drury Lane, was the last occasion I saw Dan Leno and Herbert Campbell work together. They were a great pair, and merely to see them together was a laugh, for Herbert Campbell was a man of tremendous proportions while Dan Leno was one of the tiniest. Once, I remember they played "The Babes in the Wood," and you imagine what they looked like - Herbert the huge little boy and Dan the diminutive little girl.

The "Aladdin" cast also included Ada Blanche, Decima Moore, Cinquevalli, and the Brothers Griffiths. The Brothers Huline played clown and pantaloon, and myself Harlequin, we three being sons of old Drury Lane clowns.

Great days were those for pantomime. Far be it from me to say too often "those were the days" but certainly since then pantomime has changed out of all knowing.

How many people to-day realise, for example, that a pantomime is not really a pantomime, without the Harlequinade – and how often is it seen to-day? In my father's day there were more scenes in the Harlequinade than in the opening of the pantomime. Take, for example, an old bill which I possess giving the programme of an Easter attraction at the old Effingham Theatre, in Whitechapel Road, in 1851. (Later this famous old theatre became known as the East London Theatre, then it became "Wonderland," a boxing hall, and to-day, I believe, is a picture palace.)

The star of the show was one of the most famous of clowns, Tom Matthews. Just to look at that old bill is to realise the extraordinary change which has come to this class of entertainment.

While indeed there were but three scenes in the "opening" that is, what had since become the pantomime itself, there were no fewer than eight in the Harlequinade which followed the "grand transformation scene," and before this I believe it was not unusual to have as many as fourteen or fifteen such scenes.

This old Effingham bill is extremely interesting, too, as showing what a wealth of entertainment was offered to theatre-goers in those days – and all for 3d. (gallery), 6d. (pit) and 1s. (stalls and boxes!) – and half-price after half-past eight!

Ringing up at 6:45, the bill shows, there was given a drama in two acts – the "Prodigal Daughter." Then follows a Hornpipe by a Mr. Teague, and a Buffo Song by a Mr. Willis.

Now comes the Pantomime called "Harlequin and the Three Witches, or The Magic Black Puddings," in which come the three opening scenes followed by the grand transformation scene and the Harlequinade with nine scenes and a finale "glittering in the refulgence of One Thousand Variegated Lamps!" And the performance is rounded off by a comic song sung by one Mr. Warren and concluded finally with the historical drama "King Louis XIII" or "Love's Metamorphoses."

Could one see the like of that today for 3d?

And talking of the old Effingham reminds me of a story my father used to tell of the days when he was a young man and the Effingham was owned by a gentleman of the Jewish persuasion whose culture was not quite equal to his financial qualifications.

Among other plays put on at this time was "Macbeth" and in Act 5, Scene 3, Macbeth calls, "Seaton! Seaton!" and the third call for "Seaton" is that character's cue for entrance.

The gentleman playing Seaton was waiting in the wings one night to make his entrance and when Macbeth called the first time the proprietor, who was also standing in the wings, said, "Go on, it's you, he'th calling you." Of course the man replied, "That's all right, sir."

Again Macbeth calls, "Seaton!"

The proprietor, getting worked up, said, "Go on, you, go on. He'th calling yer."

But the actor said nothing and, of course, didn't move.

Then again "Seaton!" and Seaton duly entered.

On the second morning, on going into the treasury, Seaton found that 5s. had been stopped from his salary. Indignantly he asked why, when the proprietor replied:

"You didn't know your part. Macbeth had to call you three times before you went on!"

And, despite the man's protests, he was ordered to clear out.

So Seaton at once went to the actor playing Macbeth and said, "Look, old chap, I've been stopped five shillings. I know I'm right. I don't come on till you call Seaton the third time. That's so, isn't it?"

"Why, certainly, laddie. I'll speak to him."

So, when Macbeth's turn came to go into the treasury, he expostulated and pointed out that the guv'nor had made a mistake in fining Seaton the five shillings.

"But you had to call him three timeth before he came on," said the proprietor.

Macbeth explained patiently. "Yes," he said, "but that's in the play."

"Then," said the proprietor, "who wrote this play?"

"Why, Shakespeare," said the other, astonished.

Said the proprietor, "Oh, did he?" Well, he don't write any more plays for the Effingham Theatre!"

* * * * *

What a pleasure it is now to look back on Boxing Day at Drury Lane. The long queues outside the building... the cries of the hawkers ... "All the pantomime songs!" ... the cry of the baby in arms whose mother has been holding him in the queue for two or three hours ... and then the doors are opened – the people flock in ... the murmur of excited children's voices....

The noise and the bustle of the kiddies as they find their seats ... and then ... the curtain rises ... the scent ... wonderful smell ... aroma of oranges that comes like a spray over the footlights ...

But how many of the audience spare a thought for the feelings of the artistes, putting on their make-up in their dressing-rooms? For, on a first night of panto or in fact any first night, the conscientious performer is in a state of nerves and anxiety. I have never yet met a really good artist who is not nervous on a first night. As a matter of fact, the man or woman who is over-confident and does everything at rehearsal is generally a fearful flop at the opening performance.

For this reason I have often thought what a pity it is that critics are invited on the first night, when a show is produced in a state of nervous tension that must affect it. How much better if they could be held off for a few days while the performance settles down into its stride, and when the little things that so often go wrong on a first night have all been put right and the roughness smoothed over.

But there it is. You can't keep the critics out, and many a good comedy is turned into a tragedy just because the performers were too strung up on the first night.

On these first nights of pantomime how delightful it is to watch the faces of the children as the curtain goes up. With what eagerness they follow the scene with what joy they greet every entrance as they ask each other – and this is always a leading question in the pantomime audience – "when's the clown coming on?" – How they exclaim and coo and yell when at last Joey tumbles his way on to the stage from wings or flies or anywhere!

The yells of sheer delight when he burns the policeman with a red-hot poker, or smacks the Pantaloon in the face with a string of sausages, or greases the step with a pound of butter .... knocks at the door .... and somebody skids!

A thousand such laughs there were. Alas! How different is the amusement of children today! Now it's gangsters and guns, not sausages and red-hot pokers.

But what heroes those old, great clowns were to the youngsters of yesterday.

How, for instance, the name of Joseph Grimaldi has lived. That Charles Dickens should have devoted himself to writing the life of this great clown puts him, in my opinion, among the great figures of the stage – and yet there are those who affect to despise a clown!

I for one would have given anything to have heard Grimaldi sing his famous "Hot Codlins" or "Trippety Witchett." My father taught me these songs when I was a boy, and many a time have they been useful to me, too.

There was the time when, during my first visit to France, I was invited to a party given by my brother Dick's family in Paris, and, regarded as an actor, I was naturally asked if I would do anything towards the entertainment.

I couldn't entertain them with the comic songs of the day, for I knew none of them well enough, but Dick suggested that I should sing "Tipperty Witchett" – and from that time I was a success at every party I went to, and never was I allowed to escape making my contribution with this song. And, believe me, I was always willing to "oblige".

"Tipperty Witchett" depends not so much on the words for its success as on pantomimic business and facial expression, and it became my stock-in-trade as a concert entertainment in France.

Talking of Grimaldi, I think I could not do better than quote from a very illuminating and informative pamphlet about that marvellous clown which was published by my old friend George Lupino to appeal for funds for the "Wolves," a society which was formed to help his old and broken down colleagues. Not only does George tell in brief the story of "Joey" and incidentally reveal George's tremendous admiration for Grimaldi, but it summarises too the development of pantomime and the Harlequinade which I have mentioned earlier in this story.

"Pantomimes were played many, many years before Grimaldi was born," says Lupino.

"They were short plays without words and very seldom occupied the stage more than twenty-five minutes. The Pierrot was the funny character, but rather on the sad side. Harlequin was the principal character – hence Pantomime Harlequinade.

"Signor Grimaldi was the first to make the sad pierrot into a comic one and was known as the rough and tumble pierrot. He lengthened the plays by adding two comic scenes to them.

"Grimaldi had a little son named Joey or Joe. Joey was carried on to the stage when quite a baby, and when he was four or five years of age would stand in the side wings and watch his father. He was ever ready to laugh at his father's antics and was often heard to say, "When I grow up to be a man I want to be like my dad – I want to make people laugh."

"Little Joey, as he grew older, played many parts in his father's pantomimes – the monkey, cat, dog, demon and in the stock seasons played parts in dramas, including page-boys, and various parts in Shakespearean plays. Truly a good training. He was taught to sing, dance and act, and became a splendid pantomimist.

"He was the first to bring Harlequinade up to date, and would burlesque the manners and customs of the period, particularly the dude. The dude or swell of that period wore a black wig brushed down the back and tied in a black silk bag, a small lace collar round the neck, and breeches fastened just below the knee, silk hose with cloches and bright-coloured shoes with a buckle or rosette.

"To make a burlesque of this costume, Grimaldi turned up the wig at the back, wore a large collar now called a ruffle, and pulled the breeches above the knee, making them bulge out to be used as pockets. The cloches on the stockings and the buckle or rosette on the shoes he exaggerated. He covered his costume with bright-coloured spots.

"He added six or eight scenes to the Harlequinade and when he made his appearance the audience saw he was a burlesque of the scene of that day. His face he had powdered until it was almost white; he had enlarged his eyebrows and rouged his lips until it gave him the appearance of having a very large mouth. To make him look still more grotesque he painted a funny shaped patch on his cheeks instead of the small beauty spot of the period.

"His first greeting was 'Hello! Here we are again!' and the audience received him in unbounded approval, and ever since he has been copied by other clowns and pierrots."

There indeed is the history of the clown and his costume as we know it today. And we owe it all to Grimaldi.

But that was not all that Grimaldi did. His influence reaches down to the pantomime of this very day, and in his lecture George Lupino shows how he altered its construction.

"About this time," George goes on, "the managers built up a fairy story to the Harlequinade. This fairy story was merely the opening of the entertainment, and at the end of the story a fairy would transform the play by turning the father into Pantaloon, the daughter into Columbine, the sweetheart into Harlequin, the man-servant into Clown, and the other characters into sprites.

"This was the real and old transformation – the origin of the present day transformation scenes. Since those old days the transformation of the characters in sight of the audience was done away with, and a more elaborate transformation scene was enacted which allowed time for the chief characters to change their attire with more leisure.

"The clown's 'Here we are again' was gradually added to until the pantomime clown became a speaking clown. Grimaldi then introduced little comic songs, but there was only one which was a real success, and this was written to please the children and the children only. He always worked it because it enabled the children to speak to the clown, and the clown to answer them back, just as the children do to-day. Most of this fun was centred round a butcher's shop, and the song he introduced which the children loved the best was called 'Hot Codlins.' Hot Codlins were little apples dipped in treacle and baked – now called 'Toffee Apples'."

To come to clowns nearer to my own story. There was "Wattie" Hilyard, whose last appearance was Clown in 1882 at the Theatre Royal, Covent Garden.

I never saw him play, myself, but as a little boy I remember him well off the stage. There was that time I went down to Liverpool with my father to play the Little Old Man of the Mountains and then Wattie had the Clown Tavern in Circus Street (what apt names).

When Wattie retired he came to London, and lived and died at 354, New Cross Road. A few days before his death he was visited by Henry Irving. One day when he was living in New Cross Road he was invited out to a shoot, with Charles Brown, then the champion pigeon shot, Tom Parry, and S. G. Janes. Now, Wattie had never fired a gun in his life unless perhaps on the stage now and again he had to fire off a blunderbuss.

After traipsing around the fields all day they had a very good bag, but poor Wattie hadn't shot a bird of any description. As, at the end of the day's shoot, they were returning to the farmhouse for the evening meal, and were passing a field as they walked down the country lane, Charlie (Nimrod) Brown pointed out some forty or fifty chickens running in a farmyard.

Says Charlie, "Come on, Wattie. I'll give you a shilling for every one you hit."

Now, Wattie being a rather short and stout little man, could not balance himself properly on the gate, so Tom Perry got two bushel baskets which were near for him to stand on. They lifted him on the baskets and Wattie took aim at the chickens, but unluckily pulled both triggers at once, and went head over heels off the top of the baskets, to be caught by Tom Parry.

When the casualties among the chickens were counted there were twelve dead and eight winged. So Brown had to give Wattie twenty shillings and also pay the farmer for the birds.

Among other first-rate clowns were Fred Evans, my godfather, and father of the late Will Evans; and George Lupino, father of Stanley Lupino, who was one of the most brilliant star-trap performers I ever knew.

George Lupino, indeed, was the only man who could do a double pirouette out of a star-trap, and during my first year at Drury Lane with Charles Lauri, I remember Lauri betting him it couldn't be done. We all gathered on the stage one morning before the matinee and wondered: "Could he do it?" Suddenly came the word "Go!" and a second later the trap flew open and George did the most beautiful pirouette before making a perfect landing on the stage. To-day perhaps no one would have been so interested, no one perhaps would have understood the beauty of it, or the importance of it in our lives, but then traps were important. Without a trap scene a pantomime wasn't a pantomime!

In those days to play the clown was one of the highest forms of our art; to aim to don the motley was a worthy ambition indeed. At this moment I have before me a letter from Arthur Williams in which he tells me that James Fernandez, that great contemporary of Henry Irving, made his first appearance on the London stage at the Bower Saloon, Lambeth, playing clown for my father's benefit in 1857.

In spite of the general impression to the contrary, clowns were as often as funny off stage as on it. One of the most clown-like things Father ever did was to walk on his head and hands from the Old Vic to the Lord Hill public house facing Waterloo, for a wager.

It was an odd thing that so many minor clowns came from the neighbourhood of Marylebone. But these people seemed to work pantomime only; for the rest of the year many of them were house-painting, which seems a strange combination, but nevertheless it was so. I have been told it hurt a house-painter in those days to hear the cry "Sweet Lavender," because it marked the close of the house-painting season, when the work of the painter was nearly finished for the year. One day, one of these Marylebone house-painter-clowns was on top of a ladder painting a house in Loughborough Road, Brixton, when a man in a cart passed, selling coal. As he passed the house which was being decorated he shouted up to the painter "D'you want any lavender?"

The painter-clown turned quickly towards him and said, "We don't want any slate; we've done the roof!"

But it is not everybody who despises the clown even to-day. Mr. M. Willson Disher, who has devoted a lifetime to the historical study of clowning and has written much on the subject, asked in the Evening News of April 26, 1924, "How many of our comedians could play clown?"

And goes on to answer his own question:

"George Robey would like to, and has gone so far as to be photographed in the triple-tufted wig and frilled costume. But his methods are not at all suited to a character whose humour should take the form of action, not words. Leslie Henson, though of the wrong build for clown, would make an excellent pantaloon, since he has the gift for visual fun, the gift for creating jokes out of 'properties' which caused pantomime to be called 'the wit of goods and chattels.'

"Perhaps Will Evans would give the truest representation of Joey. Like Bert Coote and Fred Kitchen, he was born in the Harlequinade, and still reminds one of it in his knowing smiles and instinct to make confusion worse confounded.

"What we lack at present," Mr. Disher points out – and I think he is right – "is the means for training clowns.

There are few low comedy parts in the plays of to-day to provide opportunities for actors to discover whether they possess the gift for raising laughter.

But whatever may be the general opinion about the pantomime of to-day, it is really sad that the clown should have fallen into so minor a part, for his is indeed a minor part when one considers what for a century he has been.

The change set in when the opening of the pantomime was lengthened and the comedians began to take over the work of the characters in the Harlequinade, doing all their tricks before the Harlequinade was due to begin. Then the proprietors who thought they must tack on a Harlequinade to the pantomime would just let anybody put on a clown's dress, down to a property man or a stage carpenter.

One of the strangest accidents that can ever have befallen a clown, I think, is one that happened to my father at the Theatre Royal, Deptford. This theatre abutted onto Deptford Creek, the canal that passes through the district; many people will remember it to-day as Dickson's Coal Walk. My father was running a show there with my uncle, Tom Lamb, and they were finishing with a Harlequinade, Uncle Tom playing clown, and dad Harlequin. When it came to the chase where the Harlequin takes the leaps, he not only leapt through the scene, but also through a window at the back of the stage and landed clean in the creek!

My father could never swim a stroke in his life, and no doubt, hampered as he was by the heavily spangled dress of Harlequin, this would have been his inglorious end, in spite of his magic wand, but Clown dived after him through the leap and pulled him out.

Which reminds me. It was to this same theatre in 1816 so I have been told and even to-day, one hundred and twenty years later, people in Deptford still delight to tell about it! that Edmund Kean, then playing at Drury Lane, rode over one afternoon to visit his old friend, Jemmy Wright, the comedian.

The two spent a happy afternoon, imbibing strong liquor – and they say it was strong – but Wright got so wrong he was unable to appear in the evening.

Kean, completely forgetting or ignoring his engagement at Drury Lane, cheerfully offered to deputise for his friend, and in due course went on to do his act.

Whether it was the strong liquor, or whether it was something else, he was such a flop that the locals, regardless of the fact that this was the great Edmund Kean of Drury Lane, would have none of him, and loudly demanded their money back! The bird!

And that was the Edmund Kean who, between 1814 and the date of his death in 1833, received no less a sum than £176,000 for his professional exertions – an interesting figure, by the way, when one hears so much of high salaries of to-day compared with those of yesteryear.

Chapter X

The end of the pantomime at Drury Lane that year, 1896/7, began yet another phase in this strangely varied life of mine.

Like all the pantomimes at Drury Lane this one was tremendously successful, but it could not last for ever and at its end was bound to arise that almost ever present question "What next?"

So I felt that it was fortunate when, returning home from a Drury Lane matinee one day, I met Jack Royal, who was then playing with the Boisset Troupe, and he told me his contract with them was finishing shortly. I suggested that we should form a partnership, work out a presentable double act, and try our luck on the Continent.

We met again on the following day and planned out our act – a bad one, I fear, made up of a song or two, a bit of dancing, and a few of what are now called "crazy gags." By the time we had rehearsed it and got it into any sort of form, the pantomime was over, and we began to look out for some engagement in which we could give it a local try-out before risking it unfledged abroad.

However, it was not so easy and time dragged on, but in the meantime Charlie Carden, with whom I had worked that short-lived Scottish tour a year earlier, had come to stay with my mother, and he said to me one day,

"I hear the Marina Music Hall at Ramsgate is closed. What about trying to fix a week there?"

So my mother obliged with the fares and we went down on the Tuesday and saw Mr. Daw, the proprietor, who agreed to share fifty-fifty with us to do a show commencing at seven and finishing at nine, when the seating in the centre of the hall was cleared away and dancing began and lasted until eleven. That was the sort of hall it was.

This sounded good enough; we were nothing if not enterprising – and the next thing to do was to find our variety bill. Well, we started by wandering down to the sands, and there we found Steve Cook, whose widow after his death years later, by the way, married Whimsical Walker.

At the time, Steve was doing a turn on the sands with the aid of the greatest novelty of the day, "Here you are, Edison's latest invention. Come and listen to it. Here you are, one penny each." It was an Edison Bell phonograph of the early cylinder type and with a listening apparatus you put to your ears like a doctor's stethoscope – and crude indeed it was, not aided by the fact that the sand would blow on to the record and get mixed up somehow with the tune!

But Steve was doing a "roaring" business, just the same, for it was the first time one of these new wonder-musical-boxes had been seen outside London.

Steve was a good fellow and when we told him how things were, he agreed to come along and do a song or two, saying, "Give me a pound at the end of the week if things are all right!" So we topped the bill with Steve Cook.

Then we discovered a local entertainer called "Sergeant Major Morris," a sort of sword-manipulator who did a double act with his wife. He, in turn, introduced us to his landlady's daughter, a young woman dying to go on the stage. We heard her sing. She had a rather nice voice but no evening dress, so I suggested that it might be a novel attraction if a somewhat daring one, if she sang her ballads in a bathing costume. She, of course, came for nothing – and only too pleased.

That made three turns. Charlie Carden did a few descriptive songs in evening dress. I remember one of them now:

"Lay him away on the hillside,
Along with the brave and bold;
Inscribe his name on the scroll of fame
In letters of purest gold;
My conscience will never desert me,
He said with his dying breath.
May the Lord bless the cause of Freedom,
For which I was sentenced to Death."

He was a very patriotic Irishman, dying for his country – and it went down very well.

Then I did a comic singing turn, and a slate-dancing act with Charlie under the name of "The Brothers Poole," and then Charlie and I finished the programme with a dramatic sketch entitled "Father and Son."

After paying all expenses at the end of the week, our first venture into production gave us the magnificent profit of £4. 10s. each!

On Sunday morning Charlie stood outside the station to wait for excursionists arriving from London. He found a couple of people not returning that day who were willing to sell him the return halves of their tickets for 1/- each. So we got home well in pocket.

Charlie, by the way, was a native of Yarmouth, and went to school with George Mozart, afterwards to become so famous a member of our profession. George, after he left school, was drummer in the band at the Aquarium Yarmouth, and I believe that was his first start.

Back in town I was lucky enough to find an old friend in the person of Jimmy Manhill, the Jester, who out of the generosity of his heart (there couldn't have been any other reason!) booked Jack Royal and me with our double act for a week in June at the Theatre Royal, Woolwich, and another week at the Palace, Hammersmith, for £5 at each hall. So we were able to try out our show. To our biased eyes, it seemed at any rate passable and we thought it might go well enough on the Continent.

So, full of optimism, we got ourselves some printed notepaper and some lithographs – without which no speciality act had a chance of being booked in those days – and sent out some two hundred letters – to Germany, France, Italy, Belgium, and in fact to every address we could find where there was a theatre.

We got one reply.

It came from a man named Cappocholio, at the Old Eldorado, Naples.

More correspondence followed and eventually we fixed a contract with him for fifteen days at 150 lire a night. It was a good price, of course, (worth about £6 a night), but I suspect that the fact that my brother Richard had played at the theatre years before and had been a great success, and also that I had the audacity to address my letters from the Theatre Royal, Drury Lane, had a good deal to do with that!

Somehow we managed to raise about £20 and started for Naples via Paris, where I stopped, naturally, to call on my Brother Dick and his French family. My partner, Jack Royal, who had never stepped outside England before, was in the seventh heaven of delight, and I think he would have stayed in Paris for ever if he could have thought of a way.

But, anyway, we stayed long enough – a matter of two days and two nights – to upset all our financial arrangements, and by the time I could persuade Jack that it was time to move on – alas! We no longer had the fare! But brother Dick, like the good fellow he was, came to our rescue, and though we had to put up with an elder-brotherly lecture, he bought our tickets through to Naples and set us up with a basket of provisions consisting of two long French loaves cut into four, two garlic sausages and four bottles of red wine. And so we were off again.

All went well, and Jack was enjoying himself tremendously in his new surroundings – until we got to the Italian frontier. There we were informed that if we wanted to go on by the express we had to pay extra on our third-class tickets – supplement they called it – or wait for a later train. By now, needless to say, we were down again to three or four francs, the loaves had disappeared, there were but two end-pieces of sausage, and the wine had vanished many, many miles before.

So we waited, and at long last boarded the Italian local train and discovered that, if the French trains could hardly be described as luxurious, third-class travelling was rather too suggestive of cattle-trucking for our liking – worse even than a rush-hour third-class from Liverpool Street to Leytonstone – and you can't say more than that!

Arriving at Milan – oh, those Italians! – once again we were told that we could not go on by that train unless we paid excess. So out we had to get.

At any rate it did give us an opportunity to look round Milan, and one thing we saw which stands out in my mind was a company of the famous Bersaglieri, the wonderful regiment which is so amazing for its training in forced marching. One hears them coming – they approach – they pass with their strange, striding step – and are gone.

Our next stop was at Genoa – and we were now down to about tenpence. Here again we found ourselves with six or seven hours to wait. And with tenpence!

So I suggested to Jack that I should try to raise a few lira on my diamond tie-pin. It was worth three or four pounds, anyway. But what was the Italian equivalent for the three brass balls? We didn't know, and our Italian was so limited that we couldn't ask. So, after some wandering and wondering, we decided to try our luck at a certain tourist office, where we should at least find someone who spoke English. We did, but he spoke it with a very German accent, and when I explained the situation, showed him our Naples contract, and asked him politely if somewhat diffidently if they could be kind enough to let us have a little money on my breast-pin and I would send the money back together with a little present for himself as soon as ever we got to Naples – he was so indignant that he practically threw us out of the place. How dared we! Well, before we left I told him how we dared – and not in Italian, either!

So we left with our ten-pence. I gave half of it to Jack and told him to go into a shop and get a bit of cheese – he could point to it, while I went to another shop and bought some bread. With our purchases, and one of the empty wine bottles which we filled with water, we trudged wearily back to the railway station waiting room, and set about it. And then we discovered we had been caught again. They had given Jack Parmesan cheese – a stone-like variety that is used for grating on to macaroni – and you couldn't cut it with anything softer than a hammer and chisel. So altogether it was a merry meal!

On again, stopping at Spezia, Pisa and Rome. At Pisa we went to the famous leaning tower, but we were too hungry to take much interest in it.

Naples. Early morning. Three-ha'pence strong. And dead tired. The journey had taken nearly three days and nights. No sooner had we touched the platform than, as though to rub it in, we were surrounded by porters who seemed to have the odd idea that everybody who looked like an Englishman must be rolling in lire.

And here for once I found the old "waxi homi" slang very useful and I was able to say and say and say "Nanti dinari."

And in case you haven't come across a "waxi homi" I should explain here that it was a slang used by the London street minstrel – the 'blacked-up' minstrel – and it had undoubtedly been developed from Italian.

Strange as it may seem, a cockney, not knowing any Italian at all, could always scramble through Italy, if he happened to know a bit of the slang and a few words of, say, French.

It is rather sad, I think, that the real "waxi" has faded out, for indeed this form of entertainment, once so popular and everyday a part of London's entertainment world, does seem to have become almost extinct.

Quite recently, however, I did happen to see two real genuine waxies in the West End, and because they seemed to carry with them an echo from the cheery past of a busker's life I spoke to them. As it happened, one of them recognised me, and when we talked of the old ways he said, "Yes, Fred, we really are the last two in London – well, the last two old 'uns, anyhow – and when we've gone....."

So another bit of old London life seems to be about to vanish for ever....

Having, with our "waxi" slang then, managed to dig our way through the horde of porters, I left Jack Royal to stand by the baggage and went out to explore Naples and find the Eldorado Theatre, where I hoped to raise enough to release our luggage, get some food, and find somewhere to stay. But all that I could discover was that it was too far to walk; as a matter of fact, it was down on the very edge of the famous Bay of Naples, so near that, as I discovered later, one could have dived from the dressing-room window into the waters of the bay.

So I took my courage in both hands, chartered a cab and went back to the station with it, proposing to pick Jack up with the baggage and then go along to Signor Cappocholio's office, where we could get enough to pay off the cab, etc. But no sooner had we got our few belongings on the cab than we were surrounded again, this time by Customs Officers who turned everything inside out and generally made a considerable fuss. They wanted us to pay duty particularly on the two hundred double-crown lithographs we had brought with us, but after a long and very difficult explanation in a mixture of French and waxi slang they eventually let us pass through the barrier.

We drove straight to Cappocholio's office in the Via Roma and were informed by the clerk in charge that M. Cappocholio had gone away for a day or two! I then told the driver to go to the Eldorado, where I found the stage manager – who happened to be a Frenchman, by name François. He settled the cab for us, loaned me a hundred lire, and then took us to a nearby hotel where he introduced us to the manager as the "two great English eccentrics!" And no doubt the proprietor believed him! We had already been flattered to see our names on the bill outside the theatre in letters at least three feet high.

The following day we went to rehearsal and found to our despair that our music was not the Continental pitch. This made things rather awkward as my partner, who had introduced xylophones into the act, had to set to work and file them all down to a proper pitch.

The opening night came and we went on about 11:45, both highly nervous. But, in spite of our nervousness, we got into the swing of the act, and were delighted and encouraged when we heard whistling from the front of the house – a whistling which increased until it was almost deafening. Never in my old days at the Canterbury, where whistling had often been the gallery way of showing approval and delight, had I heard such a reception, and so we put our hearts into it and our spirits rose. We were a success!

Next day, with the feeling of elation still upon us, we went to the theatre trusting that our splendid beginning would be repeated – and found a letter in the rack from the management which informed us that owing to our non-success the previous night, our contract was cancelled. "Please look at clause 8." Astonished and shocked, we found our French friend François and he broke the sad news to us that the whistling we had heard was really the "bird". And what a bird! We had been the flop of the evening! (I suppose the origin of that eloquent professional phrase "getting the bird" is really derived from this continental habit whistling a performer. And it may be more polite than booing, but its effect isn't a bit more pleasant, when you know what it means!)

It was a terrible blow, and, to make things worse, on looking at the bills at the front of the house, we found that already our names had been pasted out and, where the three foot letters announcing "Kitchen and Royal" had been, there were now big white spaces. We went to find Cappocholio, but without success, so we waited until the night and went to the show, managed to get in without being seen, got dressed and made up, and put our props in their places, as if nothing had happened.

But it didn't work. The stage-manager came up to us and informed us that we couldn't go on, as our contracts had been cancelled, and we weren't wanted. I informed him that we meant to go on, in spite of that, when he said, "Well, if you do, the band won't play." I told him we could do our act without the band.

"Very well," he said, "I'll have to ring down the curtain on you."

I said, "In that case, then, we'll play our act in front of the curtain. You can't do that to us."

After nearly coming to blows he went to find Cappocholio who had been in the building all the time but had avoided us. When he had gone, I said to Jack, "Now, if Cappocholio comes round, I'll pretend I'm going for him. But whatever you do, don't let me hit him."

At last Cappocholio arrived, and there was a scene. He spoke very good English and I found out years later he had been stage manager at the Old Royal Aquarium at Westminster. After a lot of palaver, and striking fighting attitudes, generally defying this and the whole of the theatrical institutions of Italy, he gave us grudging permission to go on that night and see if we got any better reception, and we were to see him again at his office at noon the following day.

We went on, and this time, luckily, we did much better. Not too well, perhaps, but at any rate there was no whistling. And first thing the next morning we went to the English Consulate. The Consul informed us that if we were not allowed to go on he couldn't do anything about that part of it, but possibly he might be able to use his official influence to get us our money. Only, could we afford to stay in Naples for six months? Because they would probably take it from court to court, and the case might take an endless time! He also told us this was not the first time he had had trouble over English artistes who had come to perform at the Eldorado, as only six weeks before two Englishmen had been in the same trouble as ourselves. These were the Brothers Saker, and years after, George Hughes, of Alexander and Hughes, told me this was so, as he at the time was working as one of the Brothers Saker.

The best thing to do, the Consul suggested, was to see Cappocholio according to our arrangement, and make the best settlement we could. So to Cappo's office we went, and after much argument, he agreed to let us work for the remainder of the fifteen days on condition we accepted 75 lire a night instead of the 150 lire arranged.

So that was that.

On leaving Cappocholio's office and walking along the main street, we ran into a group of English sailors and petty officers. I happened to say, as one will, "How are you Jack?" to one of them as we passed, and we got into conversation, and we were of course at once invited to "come and have a drink." And before we left them we had told them all our troubles, and, good lads that they were, they said, "And we'll collect some of the boys and come to the gaff tonight and give you a cheer."

They kept their word and when we went on that night we were greeted with all the rousing enthusiasm of the good old British Navy, and needless to say were so successful that we had to work all the old gags we could think of for encores.

First thing next morning, back to Cappocholio's office, and to him I said, "Well, what d'you think of last night? Did you see and hear how we went?"

"Yes," he said, "I should think so when you had half England in front!"

At last this very unsatisfactory engagement came to an end, and we decided to make for France. I went down to the docks and found an emigrant ship that was scheduled to call at Marseilles. One place seemed as good as another so, for twenty lire each, we bought two tickets to Marseilles and early one morning went aboard. That was the last I ever saw of Italy and the last I ever wanted to see of it.

Whenever I've heard anyone pull that ancient gag "See Naples and die!" I've thought of how I did see Naples, and might easily have died – of starvation!

Our ship was an emigrant ship all right, with emigrant conditions, but I found a friendly steward who for a couple of lira found us two clean mattresses and got us permission to sleep under an awning on deck. The boat was packed with Italian emigrants and for our meals we had to line up at the cookhouse door with enamelled plates and get a plate of macaroni stew, which cost us fourpence, and a penny mug of coffee. But all the same, it was really a most beautiful journey, passing down the coast of Sardinia and Corsica.

The nearer we came to Marseilles, the more our troubles fell from us, for I had been there twice before, and it was something a little more like home. As I said to my partner a dozen times, "Don't worry, Jack, we'll soon be at Marseilles. We'll get some work there!"

But we didn't. When we did arrive at Marseilles it was only to find that all the places of amusement were closed for the summer season! And though, at the little café I had been wont to frequent when I was there with the Lauri troupe, we met any number of my old French friends, they were all out of work!

However, one of them suggested that I should call and see Mr. Richard, one of the best impresarios in the South of France. I did so, and again the magic name of Kitchen worked. For being a brother of Kitchen of Kitchen and Osborne (the name that Dick and his partner used and which was known all over France) he gave me a contract on the spot to open in Algiers four days later. Also he gave us a couple of second class tickets there and then (which was really lucky) and 200 francs in advance.

But our troubles in Italy had had their effect on poor old Jack Royal and he had become very depressed and low-spirited and, on my getting back to the café, highly elated with our offer, and showing him the contract for Algiers, instead of greeting it with pleasure, he almost burst into tears, and said, "What, go to North Africa? It'll be quite bad enough having to get back from here!"

Anyway, the day came round when we boarded the General Charnzey, a boat which several years later sank in the Gulf of Lyons with the loss of everybody on board, except the purser, and among them two or three performers whom I knew very well.

Chatting with one of the officers on the boat during our voyage to Algiers, he told me that the captain was very fond of English people, and also liked to practise speaking English with any passengers who cared to talk to him. So, during the day, we were introduced. He took a liking to us, and very kindly had all our baggage moved from the second class quarters into the first. Inviting us into the saloon, he said, "Now, sit down here, and I'll send you a nice drink. I know what you Englishmen like."

And we felt like it. Visions of a bottle of whisky and a siphon of soda rose before our eyes. It was a bit of a shock to both Jack and me when the steward turned up with two cups of very weak tea!

Our fifteen days in Algiers I count among my most pleasant experiences, and this time nothing occurred to mar our pleasure – unless one counts the occasion when I fell foul of a worthy citizen who hired out bicycles.

I had hired a machine one afternoon to go out and see a bit of the country. Unfortunately I not only saw it but felt it, for I cannoned into a high bank and damaged that poor bike and myself. The man was so enraged because I declined to buy the machine, that for three nights he waited outside the theatre for me with a knife! But he didn't get me. I went out by every door except the one he happened to be waiting at, and, at long last, his patience gave out.

Chapter XI

So began a series of Continental engagements that lasted almost a year and which I look back on to-day with the greatest pleasure and interest. I am more than glad that in those earlier years I was wise enough or enterprising enough, or whatever it might have been, to seek this experience abroad. It taught me much, and I heartily and sincerely commend to every young member of our profession the idea of seeing and working in other lands.

During that year when Jack Royal and I moved about France we both garnered experience which has served us well the rest of our lives.

Perhaps we were unusually fortunate, but for this period we managed successfully to keep ourselves engaged, though perhaps I should give the major credit for that to my good friend Mr. Richards of Marseilles.

No sooner, indeed, had we concluded our fifteen days in Algiers than, on returning to Marseilles, friend Richards booked us for another fifteen days at Toulon, then at Sète and Béziers and that charming little town of Avignon.

It was here at Avignon that misfortune and trouble did perhaps threaten, but it was no more than a threat, for, when we found ourselves with a blank time ahead as we did at the end of our Avignon engagement, once again I did the daring thing and risked what was almost our last few francs on an advertisement in "L'Agence Lyrique."

This "Agence Lyrique" I had heard was owned and edited by a man named Rasimi who was also a theatrical agent. I had been given the tip that if one wanted an engagement through Rasimi one must advertise in his paper, and just how well it worked is shown by the fact that the very day after we sent our last fifty francs and the copy for the ad. there came a wire from our agent-editor offering us an engagement at Bordeaux at 75 francs a night.

I wired him back that we would accept it if he would send us 200 francs in advance – and that got us out of that little spot of bother!

When we got to Bordeaux we found that we were required to deputise for a couple of English eccentrics, O'Connor and Brady, two men well known at the time both in England and on the Continent. The stage manager was M. Morton, who was brought to London some years after by that great picker of talent, C. B. Cochrane.

Our luck held at Bordeaux, too, and we went over so well that we got an extension of seven days, making our total engagement twenty-one days.

It was here that I saw a remarkable demonstration of the wonderful efficiency of circus folk. Passing through the big square in the centre of the town one day, it was empty and deserted. Next morning on what had been that great unoccupied space was a huge building with a seating capacity of, I should think, not less than a couple of thousand people. Never have I seen such a fine piece of work done in so short a time elsewhere.

This was the Cirque Plege.

Incidentally I was delighted to see it, for always I have had a soft spot in my heart for the circus and circus people, for many of my best friends have been clowns, those stars of the sawdust ring. It isn't so very many years ago that Sir Oswald Stoll, wanting a troupe of eight circus clowns at the London Hippodrome, asked me to find them and gave me a contract, and never have I had a happier and more splendid team of men to work for me.

It did not take me long at Bordeaux to make the acquaintance of some of the circus performers and among others I got to know M. Leonard, the principal clown, and before long I was putting in as much time as I could at the circus itself and even working gags with the clowns from the ring-side (which might have been awkward if the proprietor of the music hall I was working at had known anything about it!)

But, as I have said, I had already a fair acquaintance among clowns – and I am speaking now, of course, of the circus clown as distinct from the clown of the Harlequinade, and indeed there is a very important distinction, for the two are as different in their methods and their work as, say, a clog-dancer is different from a ballet dancer.

The first circus clown whom I remember personally I met some fifty-six years ago, when I was only seven years of age – Little Sandy, at Astley's in the Westminster Bridge Road. He was a famous and excellent clown and it is interesting to note that when he was engaged, as he was later, to play clown in the Harlequinade on the stage at Covent Garden, he was not at all successful, which goes to bear out my opinion that the two classes of clown cannot successfully adapt themselves to each other's work. If the circus clown is not necessarily any good on the stage, it is equally true to say that the stage clown is just as likely to be a flop in the sawdust ring – and probably more so.

I remember three very good circus clowns whom I met on the Continent – Jimmy, Johnny and Danny Guion. Jimmy, I believe I am right in saying, was the originator of the "Auguste" of the circus ring, which was really the result of an accident.

Jimmy was engaged with a circus at Hamburg, and had to put on a dress suit to assist a man who was performing in a tank to go up a little step-ladder and hand the performer different props. One night, whether by accident or design, he tripped up on the top of the ladder and fell into the tank. Accident or not it was very, very funny, and as poor Jimmy clambered out, his dress-clothes dripping with water, he was such a ludicrous sight that the crowd yelled with laughter.

So was "Auguste" born. From then onwards every circus ring has had the famous clown in the floppy dress-suit who makes himself ridiculous to the delight of the audience.

* * * * *

I've diverged from my story, however, and must get back to Bordeaux, where, as I have said, we went over so well that our engagement was extended for a further seven days, and the end of the year found us with an engagement at the Ba Ta Clan in Paris, where we went for fifteen days.

Just at that time things were not too good in Paris, and there were a good many of our fellow pros there who were not so lucky as we were. My brother Dick, for one, was unemployed, and there were him and his wife to look after. My sister Lisette, too, was in Paris, and so was my brother Harry's little daughter. It was not easy to make ends meet!

In the weeks before Christmas we did not get many engagements; it was hardly surprising, therefore, that the few hundred francs that Jack Royal and I had managed to save were soon dissipated. Things began to look rather bleak again. They showed no immediate signs of improving, either, and towards Christmas Eve we had to fall back on that never-failing friend, our mother, asking for assistance to see us over Christmas. But we hadn't counted on the delays of the Christmas mails and so it happened that our Christmas Eve looked like being pretty meagre. Between us all that day we counted threepence!

Now, at the English bar in the Rue Geoffroy Marie – it was one of Bass's houses, called The Ship – you could get a "pony" of beer for 3d, so I suggested to Dick that I should take charge of the 3d and go down to the English bar where I might possibly meet some of our brother pros, when the camaraderie of the profession would certainly produce a little help in time of need.

We arranged that if I had any luck and was able to borrow a few francs, I would hang up my hat in the bar; if not, I would keep it on my head. Then they were all to come down to the café later in the evening, glance inside, and look for my hat. If it was hanging up they would know it was all right to come inside.

Now, here is the story of a miracle.

Dick had a little dog called Rubico, a half fox-terrier and half bull-terrier which Dick had picked up in Ghent. The dog was a great favourite of mine and he came trotting along beside me as I made for the Rue Geoffroy Marie.

While we were passing down the Faubourg Montmartre, someone in front, who had apparently been counting some money, dropped a coin, which fell with a tinkle to the pavement. Several people generously stopped and helped to search for it, but it had gone, and finally I left them searching and went on my way to The Ship, with Rubico trotting along behind.

Arrived there I spent my 3d for my pony of bitter, and as I sat there hoping that someone would come in soon, and wondering how long I could decently make one small drink last, Rubico began scratching at my leg. Then, as I put my hand down to pet him, from his mouth dropped a golden 10-franc piece! The bright little chap had picked it up and carried it along to pay the bill!

And that's absolutely true. Later, I must say, it became a popular trick with Rubico to pick up money, and he would get it from almost anywhere.

Soon afterwards three fellows I knew came into the bar. One of them was a German who was working for a French rubber firm, another a Manchester man who was in the bicycle trade, and the third a journalist on the Paris edition of the New York Herald. They suggested I should make a fourth for a game of poker, so I thought I would chance the ten francs that had so miraculously arrived on ten francs' worth of chips, which I did. After playing for about an hour I had made just about £12! I hung my hat up, and soon after the family filed in. So it was not such a bad Christmas Eve, after all, and we had a Christmas dinner the following day, which was more than we'd expected to do.

Soon after this Jack Royal and I fixed a week at the Metropolitan, London; but our turn did not go down so well in the Edgware Road as in the Rue de la Gaieté, and Jack and I decided to split up our partnership.

In the meantime, my brother Dick had fixed a contract for the Châtelet Theatre in Paris, and wrote to me to come over and join him. I was not particularly well at the time, and on going to the Chatelet with my brother for rehearsal, I collapsed on the stage.

Dick rushed me to his home and sent for a doctor, who attended me for the next fifteen days. I was in bed all this time, but the doctor allowed me to eat whatever I fancied. Slowly, however, I got worse, and at the end of the fortnight I became delirious.

I was then hurried away to the English hospital and within twenty-four hours the English doctors discovered that I had typhoid fever! They told my brother they feared that I had arrived too late, but they would do their best.

For months I hung between life and death, and I had three relapses when it was touch and go whether I recovered or not. At the time Dick was at rehearsal all day and often late into the night, but however late it was, as soon as he was free he would jump into a cab and dash along to see me. As the doctors said they could hold out no hopes whatever, he wired also for my other brother, Harry, to come over.

They told me afterwards that one night when they stood at my bedside the doctor told them that was the last they would ever see me alive. And the nurse who had been attending me and who was standing by – a Miss Roberts, a charming and beautiful girl – suggested that she should put me in an ice pack as a last forlorn hope. The doctor said he thought I was too weak to stand it, but she could try it if she liked. She did try, and in three weeks I was out of danger! That nurse saved my life.

During my convalescence, I received wonderful treatment. No-one could possibly have been treated better, and I am glad to pay this tribute to the splendid efficiency and kindness of every member of the staff there. This was the hospital endowed by the late Sir Richard Wallace, of the Wallace Art Collection fame, who also endowed a hospital for French people in Soho.

Altogether I was in the institution for about five months, and when I came out Dick insisted on looking after me. He would not hear of my trying to work for at least six weeks, so that it was well on in the year before I could do anything at all.

The Châtelet show, luckily, was a great success, and ran for eleven months. It was the largest and best fairy play I have ever seen put on the stage, in spite of its rather clumsy title, "Le Poudre de Perlin Pan Pan."

At last I joined this show, and when it was over Dick, who had done very well and managed to save a few hundred pounds out of his salary, brought me to London for a holiday, and while we were there we fixed up for a pantomime engagement at the Grand Theatre, Fulham, to play the Broker's Men in "Cinderella" and to produce the Harlequinade.

The "Dandini" on this occasion was Miss Gertie Millar, afterwards Countess Dudley, and the Ugly Sisters were played by Ben Albert and Alex Keith.

It was a very successful show, and the proprietor, Mr. Alexander Henderson, was so pleased with the Harlequinade that he asked me to tack on a shadow-pantomime, which we did, and he gave us a benefit matinee to pay for our trouble.

I could do with it! None of us Kitchens could ever keep money, and I was often hard-up, in spite of pulling in an occasional cheque for advertising commercial commodities on the stage, and "ringing them in" pretty badly at that. Thus: A man would enter with a board which said: "What to eat, drink and avoid." "D'you know what to eat, old 'un?" he'd say to the Clown. "What should I eat?" says Clown, whereat Harlequin bangs the board with his magic wand, and lo! It says "Edward's Desiccated Soups." "What to drink" is someone else's beer and "What to avoid" – just to round it off and make it a little less like advertising – "bad company." At this Clown says: "Then good-bye, that's the last I want to see of you!"

I often wondered that proprietors stood for this sort of thing; it was the comedian or clown who got the money, not the owner of the show. At the Grand that year I remember well getting two cheques one morning for £10 apiece for this blatant form of commercialism.

Chapter XII

The first link between my family and Fred Karno was forged in Brussels, away back when my brother Dick was playing there and Karno was quite a child.

Fred Karno was then apprenticed to Bob Aubrey, of the Four Aubreys, a team of horizontal bar performers.

One day little Fred was practising the bars on the stage of a theatre in Brussels and Dick happened to enter the place as poor little Karno slipped off the bar and burst into tears.

Dick went to him and saw that his hands were raw and bleeding. They had made the poor little chap work without hand pads and the resin had got into the broken blisters and must have been giving him hell....

That was enough for kind-hearted Dick. And Dick was already a big man – as important and influential a performer as he was physically fine and fit. He went to Bob Aubrey and told him that if he dared work the child again before his hands were properly healed – well, he'd be seeing him....

And Fred Karno was always grateful.

Among the young apprentice's duties just then was that of taking out Aubrey's baby in a perambulator, and he was usually given twopence to buy the child a sweet cake. Little Karno thought he knew a better use for the twopence than that, so he would purloin a few pieces of sugar before starting out, and when he got into a quiet street would grate the sugar round the mouth and on the bib of the baby so that, when they returned, Freddie still had the money and the baby seemed to have enjoyed the sweet cake!

It is a story that Fred Karno loves to tell to this day.

A friend and partner of Fred Karno's, when Fred was a young and struggling performer, was a young fellow named Ted Karno. In spite of the similarity of names, by the way, there was no family relationship.

One day during one of their rougher times they took out a guitar and mandolin and hired a boat with the idea of doing a little profitable busking on the river.

They moored outside Tagg's Island, then a popular river resort, and began to do their stuff. But they were unlucky. No sooner had the first strains of their opening melody floated over the island than an official came along and turned them away, telling them quite definitely that they didn't stand for any busking there!

Followed, of course, a bit of an argument, but the buskers lost, and Fred, as finally they rowed discomfited away, said, "Well, one day Ted, I'll buy that island – and then they'll see!"

And he did.

And that is the real story of the Karsino.

My own first meeting with Karno was when I was playing at the Royal Aquarium, in the day I have mentioned when G. P. Huntley and I went there together.

An accident had happened to a troupe of horizontal bar performers – the Four Polos. One of the quartette had had a fall and injured himself so badly that it was doubtful whether he would be able to go on again for some time.

Karno, who was then playing at the Royal Aquarium in his pantomimic sketch "Hilarity" – by the way, the first Karno sketch on the stage – was not a practised and experienced horizontal bar performer. He volunteered to take the place of the injured man and his offer was gladly accepted.

Thus I used to see Fred Karno, who later was to have so important an influence on my own career, whirling and twirling on the horizontal bar and doing all the spectacular tricks that a good "bar turn" can do.

My joining up with him came shortly after the close of the pantomime "Cinderella" mentioned in the last chapter, where I had been earning £20 a week, a princely salary to me then, not to mention the "perks" of the part.

I was at home with my mother one day when George Cragg came round, and told me that Karno wanted someone immediately. Karno was running his own company, and I went along to see him at Kennington.

His first question was, "Well, how much do you want?"

I wanted a good deal, but I hesitated as to how much I dared ask. Anyway, it was a long time to the next pantomime and a decent tour seemed to offer prospects of anything, so I said seven pounds.

"Too much," said Fred, "can't afford it."

Eventually I settled with him for £3 a week, began rehearsal and opened the following week, at Wigan!

I had been with Karno for about three months when Walter Groves, who was playing Sergeant Lightning in the play "His Majesty's Guests" we were doing then, was unable to turn up one night. Karno put me on to play the part and liked my performance so well he suggested my staying in the part for good. He later offered me a three years' contract at £5 a week, rising to £10, with the option for another three years. I accepted this, and thus began a ten years' association.

I think I may say with truth that it was during this period when I came to know Fred Karno, not only as an employer and the producer of world-famous sketches, but as an artist and a friend, that I really created for myself whatever little reputation I have enjoyed in the profession. I had some great opportunities, and I made the most of them.

One of the big hits in "His Majesty's Guests" was a sextette written by Herbert Darnley called "Six Little Burglars." I had a very good number, too, by the same clever lyricist, "Do Your Duty" and a duet, "O, Selena!" For a long time we toured the provinces with this very popular production.

It was during this time that there occurred a very important event in my life - I fell seriously in love. It began at Kelly's Theatre, Liverpool - the same theatre at which I played the Little Old Man of the Mountain as a child, but then known as the Grand.

I had gone to the theatre on the Monday morning for a rehearsal and was on the stage, the curtain being down, when I heard a voice singing in the orchestra pit. "What a lovely voice," I thought, and peered round the edge of the curtain to see if I could recognise the singer, but in the dim light could not make out who it was.

In the evening our musical director, Jacques Bruske, introduced me to a very charming and lovely girl who, he

Ella Warde

Fred as a young man

Mr and Mrs Fred Kitchen

told me, was one of the Sisters Letz, whom, I was delighted to learn, Karno had engaged for two weeks to introduce their ballad singing in the second act of the show. The two girls had been for some time with George Edwards in musical comedy and were now striking out on their own for the first time. Lou Barnard, whose name must be well known to every old-time sailor in the Navy, was the uncle of the other girl, and had got Karno to engage them for the two weeks to give them a send-off.

The girl who I admired so much was Ella Warde, and her partner, the niece of Barnard, was Sara Levoi.

Our acquaintance developed rapidly. After the two weeks were up, we corresponded regularly and kept in touch. Eventually I proposed to her in one of my letters and she decided to take a chance on joining up for life with a professional funny man – which shows that she, too, had a sense of humour.

A few months later we were married at a delightful, old-fashioned little church at Bury – the Lancashire town whose other special claim to fame is its black pudding!

About this time Fred Karno had the idea that a condensed version of "His Majesty's Guests" might find a new field on the music hall stage, and commissioned Charlie Baldwin and me to re-write it in that form.

We worked it out so that we could play it from a minimum of forty minutes up to any length, according to requirements wherever we might be, and re-christened it "The Dandy Thieves." While playing it as a music hall sketch at Bolton, Karno got Mr. Peter Lawton, of the Palace Theatre, Manchester, to come over and see it.

The result was that Lawton at once booked the sketch for a six weeks' Christmas season at the Palace. There it caught on and broke all records for the theatre. After the first night a catch phrase that I used in the show, "I'm watching yer," went all over the town.

So successful indeed was it that when we left Manchester Karno carried with him a contract for another six weeks the following Christmas with a new sketch. Moreover, in addition to these special booked-ahead engagements, we frequently returned to Manchester in between times for two or three weeks, always to play to terrific business.

In the meantime Charlie Baldwin and I had to sit down and write a new sketch for the following year, and we hit on another good idea in a sketch we called "Saturday to Monday."

This we produced at Radcliffe (of happy or unhappy memory) in a newly built theatre then under the management of a one-time "strong man", by name Testo Sante.

Incidentally, I may say that it was in the copyright performance of this sketch that I introduced my baby son – Fred Kitchen, Junior – now almost as well known as his father, at least in the provinces, to the stage, so that, like his father and his grandfather before him, he made his first appearance before the public almost before his first teeth had made their first appearance.

That opening at Radcliffe I shall never forget, for it was there that I had passed through some of the worst experiences of my early struggles. When I went down again to the old "Boar's Head", now a star instead of almost a down-and-out-and-no-account, no one was more glad to see me than the miners who once had given Wally Stephenson and me such a ready helping hand in our hard luck times. And many a story we exchanged of the days when we billed the town by night for the "Career of Crime" with "Lights o' London" posters, and then we weren't allowed to open, after all!

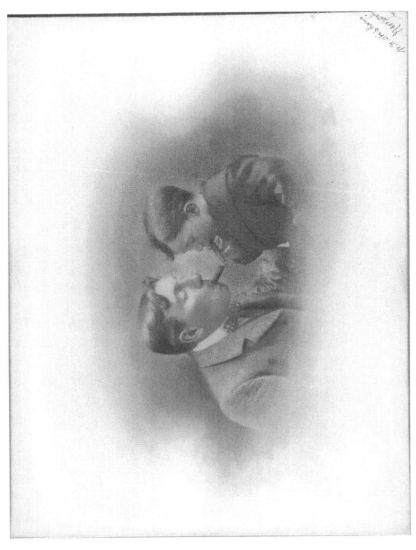

Fred with Fred Kitchen junior

In due course we took "Saturday to Monday" to Manchester and again we were a terrific success. And here occurred rather a curious thing which I have not known to happen in connection with any other play.

After we had been playing the sketch for some time, I happened to read in a newspaper that Sir George Alexander was producing a play in London with the very same title, "Saturday to Monday." I wrote to him immediately and explained that we were already playing a show under this title and that, of course, we possessed the copyright in it. And Sir George replied in a charming letter that, after all, Fred Kitchen's and Sir George Alexander's rôles were so wide apart that they would hardly be likely to clash, and that if we did not mind he would keep the title, too.

Which he did, and an odd sequel was that in a review of his play which appeared in a London newspaper, I was credited with being part author!

During this "Saturday to Monday" sketch I made acquaintance with another character of the stage in the person of Harry Lappo, whom Karno had engaged to play one of the "children" in the sketch and whom I kept with me afterwards for many years.

Now, it happened that in these earlier years I had a passion for fishing. I was nuts on it, in fact – the sort of nuts that makes a fellow get up at five in the morning, whether he's had one hour's sleep or half a dozen, just to sit on one end of a fishing line and hope for luck.

One morning I arranged with Lappo to call for me at 5:30, and off we went with our rods, tackle and parcels of sandwiches to catch the "workman's" and walk a mile and a half or so to the spot where we trusted the fish would be trustful too.

About half a mile from the pond was a little wayside public-house, and seeing the door open (this was before the days of licensing laws as we know them) we went in and got two quarts of beer in a stone jar, on which we had to leave a deposit of two shillings.

Of course, for all our good hopes, by twelve o'clock we hadn't caught anything, but we had finished up the sandwiches and the beer, and some half an hour later a little boy came and stood by watching us "fish". Lappo brightly suggested that we should take this excellent chance of replenishing the refreshment and sent the boy for some more beer.

So I said to the urchin, "Can you go to the little public house down the road there, and get us some more beer, the same as we had before? The man will know because I left two shillings on the jar."

And away went this dear, nice-looking little boy.

About half-past-three there was still no sign of the juvenile caterer and I said to Lappo, "The poor kid must have lost his way." So when we packed up, which was soon afterwards, we called in at the pub on our way back, and I said to the landlord, "I sent a little boy for some beer some hours back, but I suppose on the way back he's lost his way."

"What, was it a nice, quiet-looking little boy?"

"Yes," I said, "that's him."

"Oh, he came in all right," the man said. "He said you'd sent him to collect the two shillings on the bottle."

And I've never discovered, from that day to this, which Sunday School that nice little boy went to!

Chapter XIII

Karno was a born showman, and if anyone understood the real art of showmanship, or what nowadays some people prefer to call "presentation," he did. Never did he miss an opportunity for novel advertising.

After our successful opening in Manchester with the new sketch, "Saturday to Monday," we came back to London to play it at the Canterbury and Paragon, where once more it went over with a bang. While we were here Karno saw a chance of a fine piece of publicity that he was quick to seize upon.

An auction sale had been advertised to be held at Aldridge's in which two state coaches belonging to the Duke of Cambridge (the brother of Queen Victoria), and all the harness and equipment as well as the attendants' uniforms were to be sold.

So Karno went along and bought them, complete with all their wonderful trappings and embellishments, their coats of arms and gilded decorations.

Just then I was living in a small flat at Balham, and the night after the sale Karno decided to give Londoners a treat, so he sent along a state coach to take me to the theatre.

You can imagine the scene. A quiet suburban street, and suddenly there arrives this magnificent equipage, fit for a king, and complete with its splendid and imposing postillions. It stops before my door. Windows are flung open, and a crowd begins to gather. Curious urchins gape and stare. "Blimey, it's the Queen!" "Grr! It's Cinderella!" And the footmen ceremoniously lower the steps and stand like statues awaiting me.

Then, while the awed crowd stand and wonder, out comes ME, made up like a loud and blatant bookmaker for the wedding scene in "Saturday to Monday," grease paint and all, and as the flunkeys in scarlet and gold salute me, I climb majestically into the fairy coach and drive away amid cheers and laughter.

Then to Coldharbour Lane, Camberwell, where, with equal state and dignity, I pick up my leading lady, Miss Cossie Noel.

From then on our progress was like a Jubilee procession along a royal route. On London Bridge the police (by mistake, no doubt!) held up the traffic for us to pass. Soldiers and sailors saluted us. Passers-by gazed with respect and stood with bared heads. And steadily the crowd of urchins following on behind grew larger.

As we reached Aldgate, all the butchers ran out of their shops and banged their cleavers in respectful salutation. Customers forgot their business and flocked into the street to watch us go by.

Finally we pulled up at the Paragon. Down from the back of the coach jumped our liveried postillions again, to let down the steps, while quickly the crowd formed an avenue that left us only just room to make our triumphant way into the theatre.

Fred as The Bookmaker

Then said one urchin, who no doubt had expected to see at least the King and Queen, "Why, blimey, Bert. Look it's only Bill Bailey!"

Many times did Karno put these gaudy and glamorous coaches to good use, and invariably they gathered their crowd to add to the fame and reputation of Karno and his companies. But the best example of how they could attract the attention of a whole town was when, the following Christmas, Karno was producing a pantomime at Sheffield.

To give the show a boost in advance, he decided that he would send down one of these coaches and let it parade the town. So one day he dressed one of his girls as Cinderella, placed her in the coach, and, in the busiest hour of the day, when all the works and the factories were pouring out their work-people for dinner, the gilded equipage - now really "a fairy coach" - set out from the theatre.

Before it even started the crowd that gathered almost threatened to prevent its movement, and as it passed along street after street, so the multitude grew until, by the time it had reached the Town Hall, Cinderella and her "fairy coach" had attracted such a large concourse of people that it was literally impossible to move another step.

Traffic was held up in all directions. Police sought in vain to make a way for the coach. But the people pressed about in such a solid mass that it was only after an S.O.S. had been sent to the police station, and a special squad had been called out, that finally a way was cleared for the vehicle to make a slow but triumphant progress back to its stables.

Karno of course was summoned for obstruction, but, although he was fined some nominal amount, what cared he? It had been the most sensational advertisement for a pantomime that Sheffield had ever enjoyed.

Truly Karno was a very Barnum among showmen, for at the same time as he was giving Sheffield a thrill, he was arranging for an equally spectacular stunt to put over a new sketch called "Jail-Birds" which he was producing with his principal company in London.

For this he actually bought from the prison authorities an old and discarded "Black Maria" and every night during the run of the piece, this "Black Maria" would drive to the stage door of the theatre where the sketch was being played - and frequently we were doing two or three different halls a night - and there, to the delight of everybody within range, the "warder" would descend, unlock the vehicle and release a number of "convicts".

The "convicts" who, of course, were the actors playing parts in the sketch, were realistically made up in correct convict dress complete with broad arrow and forage cap. It was undoubtedly a thrill for the spectators to watch them marshalled by their guard and marched in as through prison gates, while the ominous and dismal "Black Maria" would wait outside for their return as though to guard against their possible "escape," surrounded naturally by an inquisitive and admiring crowd.

Yet another bright idea of Karno's, which he exploited in the provinces until it got him into trouble with the authorities, was the sending up of a balloon from which handbills announcing the show could be poured down to float into the hands of the people thronging busy streets - for always, of course, Karno picked the business hours for his stunts.

It was at Wigan that he came up against the authorities with this particular trick, for - either by accident or design a hook which "happened" to be trailing from the balloon "happened" to catch in the overhead wires of the local tramway system.

The Wiganites did get a thrill, for if you've ever seen anything dropped across a pair of overhead cables carrying thousands of volts of power you can imagine the firework display!

The whole tramway system was dislocated and traffic all over the town held up. And Karno was summoned again for obstruction and again fined.

But again, what did he care? Publicity pays!

Not only was Karno a man capable of producing brilliant ideas, but he was also a man who could accept ideas. Not for him was the foolish but all-too-common attitude of thinking that because he was "the guv'nor" he had to be everything and do everything.

For example, I remember how he said to me one day, "It's getting pretty near our time for Manchester again, Fred. Thought of anything for a new sketch yet?"

I had to admit that I hadn't, but I had just seen 'In Dahomey' at the Shaftesbury Theatre, and it had at least given me the germ of an idea. 'In Dahomey' was a musical play in which all the characters were coloured people and it proved a great success. Two coloured actors particularly, "Williams and Walker," had impressed me. They were the rage of the season.

So I said to Karno, "I have got an idea. How about a sketch in which all the characters are Jews, and me the only Gentile? I haven't thought out a plot yet, but we could call it 'Moses & Son.' That ought to go"

"Fine," said Karno. "You write it."

So pleased was he that he thereupon added £50 to a cheque he was just then writing for my Share of the authorship of "Saturday to Monday" as an acknowledgment of the bare idea.

Thus "Moses & Son" was born. In due course, the three of us - Fred Karno, Harold Garry and I - wrote the script and we began rehearsal down at the Victoria, - the same Old Vic that has been so closely connected with my story throughout.

The selection of the cast, however, was a bit of a problem. Karno put an advertisement in one of the Jewish papers and applicants were to apply at the Victoria. Hundreds turned up, and though the cast for the new sketch was a fairly large one, - running to about sixty people, - there were enough would-be and had-been performers in the theatre that day to have cast a dozen such sketches, - and to have provided the audience as well.

It was a bit of a business disposing of those we couldn't use! But eventually they were persuaded to go away and we got on with our first rehearsal.

Even then I, for one, was never allowed to forget that I had selected Jews for our characters. Hardly had I arrived in the theatre for the first rehearsal than one of the young men called me aside and sold me a cigarette holder! A few minutes later, a handsome young Jewess cornered me, asked me if I was married, and, when I blushingly admitted that I was suggested that I should take a few blouses home with me to show to my wife! I don't think there was an actor among the whole sixty who wasn't in some business or other!

We were a good company, and "Moses and Son" was one of the most successful sketches I ever played in, or Karno ever produced. It was popular with the Jewish race themselves, too. When we came to the Holborn Empire to open there with it for a month, on the first night the theatre was packed to overflowing with Jews, who, I honestly believe, had come with the full expectation that they were going to see a show burlesquing their religion and their race. What they would have done about it I don't t know; but I do know that they went away delighted, for the sketch had been written in anything but a hostile spirit.

There was one day in the year, however, when their religion presented us with a bit of a problem, - namely, the Jewish Black Fast. On that night the whole company downed props. Fred Karno, always equal to the occasion, replaced them with night-valets, chauffeurs, horse-minders, wardrobe-women, scenic artists and property men who all became actors for the night. A handbill was slipped into the programmes, which read as follows:

EMPIRE PALACE, CROYDON,.

Friday, September 28th, 1906.

The Management beg to announce that owing to its being the BLACK FAST OF THE JEWS, "Moses and Son" will, for this evening only, be presented by Christians.
The original company will appear tomorrow evening.

* * * * *

As a real honest-to-God cockney I had always prided myself on knowing something about that wonderful cockney language – "rhyming slang;" but there was a fellow in this show called Lou Benjamin who frequently came out with examples of it which I hadn't heard before.

One night, for instance, I arrived in the dressing-room to find Lou looking a bit queer. "What's the matter, Lou?" I asked. Said he: "I've got a fearful Drury Lane in the Marie Corelli."

He was full of this slang, and through him, I relearned the language. How important a place it takes in cockney speech everyone knows, and wherever light-hearted Londoners meet, there you will be sure to hear something of it.

Charles Austin and I, for example, got into the habit of talking that way, until, to a stranger, our conversation must have sounded like sheer nonsense. Charlie and I had many things in common, but perhaps most of all this fact that we were both Cockneys.

About the time of which I am writing we appeared very frequently on the same bill, although he was not connected with the Karno companies, and week after week we would travel from town to town together.

I can laugh now at the mystifications writ large on the faces of strangers in, say, refreshments rooms of railway stations, as we cheered up an otherwise dull interval between trains with some hilarious conversation in rhyming slang.

So rarely have I ever seen any of this quaint conversation put on record that I am tempted to note down here what I can remember of the vocabulary. Many of these phrases will perhaps be familiar to the reader, but I feel that there are probably very few to whom some of them will not be new.

Here they are:

Arms............ Chalk Farms
Bad............... Sorry and Sad
Bar................ Bazaar, or Jolly Jack Tar
Bed............... Uncle Ned
Beef.............. Stop Thief
Bird.............. Richard the Third
Boy............... Hobble-de-Hoy, or San Toy
Bob............... Touch me on the Nob
Bank............. Tank
Bloke............ Heaps O' Coke
Brandy......... Jack the Dandy
Breath.......... King Death
Band .... Silver Sand
Brother .... One and t'other
Belly............. Derby Kelly or Marie Corelli
Beer.............. Pig's Ear
Boots............ Daisy Roots
Can............... Peter Pan
Cards .... Wilkie Bards
Cheese .... Stand at Ease
Collar........... Holler, boys, holler!
Comb........... Miners' dream of Home
Coppers....... Grasshoppers
Cigar............ La-de-dar
Clock............ Dickory Dock
Coat .... Steamboat, or I'm afloat
Dog .... Leap Frog
Door............. Rory O'More
Dollar........... Oxford Scholar
Drink .... Tumble down the sink
Ear................ King Lear

Eyes .... Mince Pies
Face .... Jem Mace, or Chevy Chase
Feet .... Plates o' Meat
Fight .... Read and Write
Fire .... Anna Maria
Fish .... Broken Dish
Gin .... Brian O'Flynn
Glasses .... Lancashire Lasses
Gloves .... Turtle Doves
Guts .... Newington Butts
Hands .... German bands
Hair .... Barnet Fair
Hat .... Tit for Tat
Head .... Loaf o' Bread
Heart .... Jam Tart
Kids .... God forbids
Legs .... Scotch pegs
Look .... Butcher's hook
Man .... Pot and pan.
Matches .... Colney Hatches
Milk .... Charlie Dilke
Missis .... Stolen Kisses, or plates and dishes.
Money .... Bees and honey
Mouth .... North and South
Neck .... Bushel and Peck
Nose .... Fireman's hose, or I suppose
Pain .... Drury Lane
Paper .... Linendraper
Penny .... Kilkenny
Pillow, ... Weeping Willow
Pinched .... 'Arf inched
Plate .... Never too late

Pocket	Sky rocket
Road	Frog and Toad
Room	Birch Broom
Rum	Finger and Thumb
Sack	Tin tack
Sailor	Merchant Tailor
Shave	Mariner's Grave, or Dig in the grave
Shirt	Dicky dirt
Sick	Uncle Dick
Slavey	Plates o'Gravy
Sleep	Bo-Peep
Smell	William Tell
Soap	Band of Hope
Socks	Almost Rocks
Son	Hot Cross Bun
Stairs	Apples and Pears
Steak	Joe Blake
Suit	Whistle and flute
Tale	Daily Mail
Tanner	Lord o'the Manor
Tie	Peckham Rye
Time	Bird Lime
Trousers	Round the houses
Waistcoat	Charlie Prescott
Waiter	Hot potato
Wash	Lemon Squash
Water	Fisherman's Daughter
Whisky	I'm so frisky
Wife	Trouble and Strife
Window	Burnt Cinder
Words	Dickey Birds

And now, at last it seemed, I was "getting on." Thanks to good luck, ripening experience and wonderfully good friends and colleagues I was really beginning to feel that I was making a mark and that, if luck continued, my hard times were over.

I was even beginning to look back on those early struggles and hardships of mine with an interest bred of the thought that if, while they lasted, they had been unpleasant they had been equally valuable in widening my experience and qualifying me for later success. I could honestly say I was glad I had "been through the mill."

Times had changed. My name was beginning to be known and my performance enjoyed wherever we went - and there were few music halls in Great Britain and Ireland which I had not by this time visited.

The Press, too, were being very kind to me. Whenever and wherever Karno or a Karno show was mentioned I think I generally came in for honourable mention, and I can honestly say that never once in all those Karno years - or for that matter since - did I receive anything but praise from the newspapers or the general Press.

I credit Fred Karno for this happy fact as much as I do my own work and good luck, for if I was able to interpret my parts happily it was made easy for me by the fact that Fred Karno produced his shows so wonderfully. A new Karno sketch indeed was a new entertainment and a new source of delight, and everywhere it was greeted as such.

Chapter XIV

These were the days when I was coming more and more to realise the value of the comradeship and good fellowship of the variety stage.

While I was establishing myself in the public eye as a comedian, moving from town to town and bill to bill, naturally I was becoming more and more closely acquainted with my contemporaries of the vaudeville stage. A score of friendships began at this time which have lasted the rest of my life or until those friends have, one by one, taken their final curtain. But most of them, I am glad to say, are still doing their bit to make the world a brighter place to live in.

One of my life-long friends, for instance, was Joe Elvin. We had been school-friends, but it was in these earlier vaudeville days that we really got to know each other intimately.

Joe was always fond of a bit of racing. One evening he said to me, "Fred, come round to my place in the morning, and we'll have a little drink and a smoke in my office and back some winners over the 'phone. I've got a good tip for a good outsider in the first race."

So the following day I went along to Joe's place, and he said, "Now, it only wants ten minutes and they'll be off. We've got ten pounds each to win this one in the first, a ten pound each double, and a five pound each treble."

We waited anxiously. Then, when we judged the result would be out, Joe rang up the bookmaker.

We had won, and the price was ten to one.

So as we had now won £100 each clear, and £100 each to go on another horse, and another £50 each of the bookmaker's money to go in our treble, I thought wisdom would be the best policy and suggested to Joe that we had had a very good day and should finish at that.

"What!" Joe exclaimed indignantly, "is that how you bet, Fred Kitchen? Here we've got a chance to show them. Why, by to-night we can have the bookmakers crying for mercy. I feel it in my blood! And you want to cry off!" His indignation was tremendous.

So we bet and increased the stakes race after race. First the double went down and then the treble.

At the finish of the day we had lost £70 each! So the only tears that were shed that night were those we dropped ourselves!

But Joe and I were really attached to each other, and it would have taken more than that to upset our friendship.

Whenever we were playing in the same hall, or even in the same town together, we would meet in one dressing-room or the other - usually mine - after the show for a little drink and a talk.

I used to travel, as most of us do, a number of glasses among my props for this sort of occasion, and one of them was a particularly cheap and ugly product that I had picked up somewhere, but which Joe always liked to use.

So, although otherwise I might have thrown it away, I kept it for years just for his benefit.

Joe would rarely come into my room without being loaded with a "bottle" in each pocket - he used to call them 'relays' though I never quite understood why - and as he entered he would invariably remark, "Come on, old Fred, where's my glass?"

Then at one time when we had come to the end of a long London engagement, and I was not likely to encounter him again for some time, I thought I would make him a formal present of his glass. So I had a special base made for it - a particularly heavy one so that the glass couldn't easily be upset - had it engraved "Joe's favourite glass - from his old pal, Fred," and duly presented it to him as a farewell gift.

On the Sunday morning, before leaving, I called round to see Joe, and I found him very upset, and engaged in 'telling off' a servant girl. As I entered his room he was saying, "You can pack your box: here's a month's wages for you, and you can clear out!"

The poor girl was in tears before him, and Joe told me, almost in tears himself, that, in spite of the non-spillable base and everything else, the girl had managed it somehow, - she had knocked it over and broken his precious glass.

Another interesting personality whom I came to know pretty well about this time was Alec Hurley, one of the best coster comedians I have ever seen perform. There was an originality about Alec which put him right in the front rank, and with his natural neatness and smartness he was a remarkable contrast to his brother Ted, a frank, happy, natural Cockney, who gave me some of the best laughs of my life.

Just before this, for instance, during the Boer War, Alec was staying in a first-class hotel in one of the provincial towns and one night after the show he took his brother Ted in for a final drink. They got into conversation with a dear old gentleman who was also staying in the hotel, and, naturally enough, it was not long before the talk came round to the subject of the war.

"It's a shame," the old gentleman remarked, "that this war should have come about at all, because there's not the slightest doubt that the Dutch were the first to colonise South Africa, and this little country of ours, directly they see another flag planted in a place and it becomes prosperous, want to tear it down and stick up a Union Jack."

Alec's brother, very patriotic, took umbrage at this. In his strong Cockney accent he remarked, "Well, I don't know. I reely fink we're as much entitled to Sahf Africa as any blinkin' Dutch."

Whereupon Alec, who at times liked to be very "refined" said, "Now then, leave off Ted, and let us hear what the gentleman is saying"

And the old man repeated again, more emphatically, "I really think this war should never have been allowed. It should be stopped. It is absolutely the ruination of the Empire."

Ted could repress himself no longer. "Well, gaw-blimey," he jerked out, "it ain't done no good to the Alhambra, neither!"

One day I met Ted Hurley in the street and he said, "Hello, Fred, when are you coming along to see me? I've got the bars now at the Ring."

Remembering the Ring in the Blackfriars Road and knowing perfectly well that it was not licensed, I asked, "What d'you mean, Ted, the bars?"

"Oh, only tea and cawfee, yer know."

A little later I did go to the Ring, and before the boxing started I looked up Ted for a little chat and asked him how he was doing.

"All right," he said, "the only trouble is I can't get me cups and saucers quick enough. They sit there watching the fight and drinkin' their tea and cawfee out o' the spoons."

"Well, the only thing to do," I suggested, "is to get more cups and saucers."

"No, it's all right," he said. "I've arranged everything all right."

"Well," I asked, "what did you do?"

"Oh, that's all right," he said, with an air of triumph, "I've made holes in all the spoons."

Besides being the spontaneously witty and amusing fellow that he was, Ted Hurley was one of the most generous of men. I remember being at this same Ring one evening when we were getting up a list for an old performer who was just then having a rough time.

As I sat watching the boxing a man sitting behind me - one of the wealthiest people in our profession, a man who in fact had retired - tapped me on the shoulder and passed me ten shillings and said, "Put that on your list, Fred, but don't put my name down."

A few minutes later Ted came up to me and said, "Wait till after the last fight, Fred. I want to see you particularly."

I waited, and after the final bout of the evening he came to me and handed me a guinea in sixpences, shillings and coppers and said, "Put that on your list, Fred - 'from an old pal, Ted'." I have always thought that probably was the whole of Ted's taking for the day. What contrasts we find in our profession - some have lots and some have none - but, as I have said earlier, generosity is the rule, and stinginess the exception.

Just one more story I feel compelled to give about the lovable Ted. I was standing at the side of the stage at the Empire, Nottingham, one night listening to Tom Childs, the Yorkshire baritone. He was working under considerable difficulty that night for he was suffering from rather a bad cold, and when he came off he remarked that he did not think he would be able to play again during the week as his chest was so bad.

I suggested that he should ask the landlady, when he got back to his digs, for some camphorated oil and rub his chest with it - a good old-fashioned remedy that I had always believed in.

But Ted, who was standing by, thought of another idea. "Nah, I'll tell yer what ter do," he said. "Send a call-boy out for two-pennuth of Friar's Balsam, and when you get 'ome to-night, git a jug o' boilin' water, put all the Friar's Balsam in the boilin' water, put a towel over yer 'ead, open yer mouth well over the top o' the jug and then - ignore it. And then you go to bed and ex-pires"

Ted died only a little while ago, poor chap, and a friend who went to see him a day or two before he passed away said he was as cheerful as ever. My friend asked him if he was comfortable in the hospital and he replied, "Yus, all right. We get brightened up 'ere; there's a kind young feller comes along and plays the uka-daily."

Another friendship which ripened in these happy days was that with T. W. Barrett, a very funny comedian who originated what I call the "stand-still" style. Barrett was billed always as "the nobleman's son," and he died quite recently, aged, I think, eighty-four.

I remember T. W. Barrett first some fifty-six years ago, when he lived in a little house facing us in the Hercules Road. He had a famous song called "I don't like London," which was afterwards used by W. S. Penley in "The Private Secretary" when he played the Rev. Robert Spalding, and is used to this day whenever "The Private Secretary" is revived.

Barrett was engaged as principal comedian at the Gaiety Theatre nearly sixty years ago, and had he been able to fulfil the engagement might have achieved even greater fame than he did, but unfortunately poor Tommy's education was not equal to it and he was unable to learn his part. His earlier years had left him no time for schooling and up to that time he had not learned to read and write, and consequently had to depend on his wife to read him his parts and even teach him the words of his songs.

T. W.'s wife was a fine, big, handsome woman, and he was a tiny, rather insignificant-looking man. They did, indeed, make an odd pair - the very picture of the hen-pecked husband that the comic artist loves - and I well remember one incident that occurred which would certainly have borne out that impression.

Tommy used to drive a very smart pony and trap, and regularly he and his wife would go for a spin in the afternoon. One day just as they drove past our house Tom by some mischance collided with a Pickford van, and was shot clean out into the road with his weighty wife on top of him.

She picked herself up in fury and, not stopping even to ask him if he was hurt, laid about him with her parasol, giving him a first-class hiding, while the crowd held their sides and roared with laughter.

Poor Tommy!

But Tom, despite his diminutive size, was very game.

One night, when he was at the height of his success, he entered the bar of the old Trocadero Music Hall (which stood on the site of the present Trocadero Restaurant in Shaftesbury Avenue) when a certain earl asked him if he would have a drink.

Being an independent sort of man, Tom declined and ordered himself a bottle of champagne. A few moments later his wife happened to come into the bar, and as she passed, the earl, not knowing who she was, made a too-familiar remark and slapped her playfully.

That was enough for Tom. His temper flamed up in a second and without a word he picked up the champagne bottle, and crashed it on top of the nobleman's head, cutting it open with a wound that must have been eight or nine inches long.

I doubt if the noble earl ever spoke to another strange lady that way!

Speaking of the old Troc reminds me of the church which stands nearly next door. It is, I think, one of the smallest churches we have in London, if not indeed the smallest. One of the truest clergymen it has been my lot to know has the living now - the Rev. Clarence May.

Years ago he was at Hackney and next to his church he had a mission hall with a proper stage, scenery, and seating accommodation for a good number of people. On Sundays when he had finished his sermon and the church service was over, many of the members of the congregation would flock into the mission hall where he would provide a very pleasant Sunday evening entertainment.

Often he would ask well-known theatrical and vaudeville artists to go down and do something, and so far as I know, they always agreed readily. There, for example, I met Violet Vanbrugh entertaining the congregation.

The first time I went there myself he said, just before I went on, "Now, Fred, I know you will be careful what you say." To which I replied, "You don't think I would do anything on a Sunday and in a mission hall like this to offend any of your people?"

"No," he said, just a trifle doubtfully, "but ....."

I went on and told a few stories. Mr. May was standing quite near and as much as I could I watched his face. He was obviously enjoying everything — until I came to the story of the two bookmakers arguing about religion.

The story was that one bookmaker was saying to another, "I'll bet you a tenner you don't even know the Lord's Prayer." And the other bookmaker says, "Done; I'll bet you a tenner I can say it,"

They produce their tenners.

Then the second bookmaker starts: "The Lord is my Shepherd; I shall not want...."

"That's enough," says the first bookmaker. "You've won. I didn't know you knew it."

When I started that story, the "Rev's" face was a study. I really think he thought I was going to say something shocking – but I've no doubt he knows variety performers better now....

In spite of the attitude of some of the clergy towards the stage, and particularly towards the music hall (fortunately and, as I think, sensibly, not now by any means so antagonistic), it has been my good luck to meet a good many open-minded clergymen during my career, and of many different creeds.

Once while travelling over to Dublin I met a Roman Catholic priest on the boat. He asked me if I was going to the Curragh races, but I explained that I shouldn't be able to do so. However, during the journey we became very well. acquainted and he promised to come and see me at the theatre in Dublin.

He did come. He saw the show and afterwards came round to my dressing room and we had a little drink and a talk.

"I wish you could have been at the races to-day, Fred," he told me. "You would have backed a few winners."

"Did you win, Father?" I asked him.

His reply staggered me. "Yes," he said, "just a little five hundred pounds!"

Later I discovered that most of this money went to the poor in his parish - but I have often wondered how he balanced things up when he had a losing day!

Another good friend whom I came to know in those early Karno days was George Graves. George is another of those natural, spontaneous comedians who is bound to hand you out a laugh wherever you meet him.

This is the sort of thing that would happen with George. We met by accident one day on the front at Brighton. Said George immediately, "Good old Fred. Come on, we'll have some oysters."

We had some oysters, and a glass of white wine, and then George said, "Fred, have you ever seen a lobster stand on its head?"

"No, I haven't" I said. "Don't be silly."

"It isn't silly. Come along; I'll show you."

So he took me along to the big fishmonger's shop at the back of the Town Hall.

"Have you any live lobsters?"

"Yes, Mr Graves."

"All right. Bring me two or three."

When they came George put them on the slab, stood them on their heads, holding down the back tail-like part, and then in some curious way tickled them with his fingers up and down the back and then let them go. Slowly they rose vertically until they stood neatly on their heads like crustacean acrobats and then, as they seemed to recover from George's mesmeric tickling, fell flat again.

"Try it sometime" said George.

When I first met George at a pantomime at the Theatre Royal in Manchester, he was playing a comparatively small part, but already he was "going over." The town was giggling over a saying of his, "I want to see the bull-ox!"

Only recently my son, Fred Kitchen, Junior, was touring with George in a revival of "The Merry Widow," with Fred playing Prince Danilo and George in his original part.

They opened the tour at Morecombe and Fred, at any rate, was nervous and worried. It was a big part to him. When it came fairly near to time to be getting to the theatre he and George, who had been spending the afternoon together, found themselves stranded some distance away, and with the buses all packed and not an empty taxi to be picked up anywhere. Fred, as he told me later, began to get the wind up.

Not so George Graves. "That's all right, Fred; we'll get there somehow," he said.

And they did. For just then a car drew up at the kerb. In it were a man and his family. Without any hesitation George went up to him, introduced himself and Fred, explained their dilemma and said, "I'm sure you wouldn't mind obliging us by driving us along to the theatre, and when we get there we'll oblige you with a couple of seats!"

And such is the power of personality, the stranger left his family behind and "obliged".

I have always thought what a similarity there was between the personalities of George Graves and another very fine comedian whom I remember even as a boy, Fred Williams, brother of the more famous Arthur Williams, of the Gaiety Theatre.

Both of them were good friends of mine. Arthur, particularly, always took a great interest in me in those days when I was "getting on" as a comedian. One time I was playing in one of the Karno sketches at the Grand

Theatre, Clapham, and he brought Arthur Collins from Drury Lane especially to see me.

After I had been on the stage about fifteen minutes, Williams told me afterwards, Collins turned to him and said, "Yes, he's very good, this man."

Arthur said, "I told you he was good; that's why I brought you to see him. And I'm sure he's just the sort of comedian you want for pantomime," and added as an afterthought, "You know him very well; he played at the Lane years ago."

Said Collins, "What did he play? I can't fix him," no doubt thinking I had played a comedy part.

And Arthur said, "Why, he was your harlequin."

Which for some reason put Collins off to such an extent that he immediately remarked, "Oh, well, no, I don't think he'd do for pantomime."

A conclusion which has always puzzled both Arthur Williams and me. But I suppose Collins thought a good Harlequin couldn't really be a good comedian!

Talking of the Williams brothers, I cannot refrain from telling a story of Fred Williams and Arthur Binstead – "Pitcher" of the "Sporting Times."

Fred was playing in one of his sketches at two of the London halls. "Pitcher," who had a great admiration for Fred, called in early one evening to see him. Fred suggested that they should drive together to the next hall he was working.

They naturally took a little refreshment on the way.

As they drove along through one of the poorer districts of the town Fred said to Binstead, "Are you fond of jellied eels?"

"Yes, I've often had them on the racecourse, and liked them."

"Good," said Fred. "I'll pull up at a little place I know where they have the finest jellied eels in London."

They entered the shop and took their seats at the counter and the "Pitcher" (who related the story later) noticed a young girl who stood behind the counter was crying.

"Good evening, Annie," said Fred. "Give us two nice sixpenny basins of the old jellied."

The girl, between sniffs and suppressed sobs, served them, and the two, tactfully avoiding any embarrassing questions to Annie, set to.

"What d'you think of the flavour? Aren't they lovely?" Fred demanded after they had settled well down, and in between spitting out the eel-bones.

"Fine," agreed the "Pitcher" and they ordered another two basins.

By this time it struck Fred that Annie was really in some sort of trouble and so he said at last, "Well, what's the matter, my girl? What are you crying for?"

Her sobs burst forth anew. "It's about father, sir."

"About your father? Why, what's the matter with your father?" Fred ejected another bone.

"Well, sir, mother found he'd been gambling and lost a lot lately and the other night when we'd shut up shop mother went to bed and left father sitting in the little back parlour. She must have dozed off, sir, because when she woke up in the middle of the night she found father wasn't in bed."

"Well," queried Fred, as he tipped up the basin to his mouth and swallowed with obvious enjoyment the last of the jelly.

"Well, sir," the girl went on, "she went downstairs and father wasn't anywhere to be seen, and so she went out to the backyard where we keep the jellied eels in a big tank and there was father, with his legs sticking out of the tank. He'd committed suicide in the jellied eels!"

Exit Fred and the "Pitcher" – hurriedly!

Chapter XV

It began to look as though I should be playing funny parts in Karno sketches without another break for the rest of my life, and indeed I'd almost begun to think so, when Fred Karno had the bright idea that if I could keep audiences rocking with laughter as a man, I might do it ever better as a woman.

So one day, towards the end of that year, 1906, he said, "Fred, what about going into skirts and playing the Dame in pantomime?"

Variety is the spice of life, they say, and I was nothing loath, - though I must admit I was not altogether confident that my chief's high hopes would be realised. Out of all the characters I had played, never had one of them been in skirts, and I had seen enough people do the wrong thing in this guise to know that it might not be easy to do the right.

Frankly, I was nervous, for, as I say, I knew well enough how careful a comedian must be in playing a female part. The lines must be most carefully handled to avoid giving offence. Always it has been my definite principle to keep my humour clean; I have a hearty distaste for the class of joke that depends on salaciousness or double meanings on the stage, but I knew the game well enough to realise that these things might easily creep in unless the part was very carefully watched.

So that, when it came to reading and rehearsing my part, I was as critical as a Watch Committee on a Sunday evening. Consequently from that point of view my performance finally went over on that Christmas Day without a touch of anything to which the most captious could take exception.

The pantomime itself was "The House That Jack Built" and Karno produced it at the Grand Theatre, Glasgow, that season, with all the art and excellence which made his productions, of whatever kind, a foregone success.

Not that this looked like being such a success. For I shall never forget the trials and tribulations of rehearsal. Nothing would go right, and everything went wrong, and finally the dress rehearsal was a veritable nightmare.

We began at half past five in the evening, and struggled on - nobody doing anything that seemed anything like anything. Over and over our parts we went, until feet were weary and tempers touchy. At midnight we were no happier. At two in the morning, it was worse. At four I turned it up and went home, tired out and miserable. I couldn't sleep for thinking of the flop the show was sure to be.

We were due to ring up on a matinee at two o'clock. I was at the theatre early, harassed and worried - and so was everybody else. We knew it was going to flop - and I could see such reputation as I had so painfully built up gone for ever....

The curtain went up....

It was a marvellous show. Not a hitch. Not a line, not a scene out of place. It was one of the greatest successes of my life, and next day the papers were full of praise for Karno, for me, for the show, for everybody in the show.

Such, they say, is life ..... It made me feel like the old man who said he'd had a lot of worries in his life - but most of them never happened!

In fact, everybody was delighted, and we settled down for a long run. Actually it proved to be one of the longest pantomime runs I remember, for we played at the Grand for no fewer than fourteen weeks and then moved across the road to the Empire for another two weeks. We then condensed it into a one hour show and toured the music halls with it just as successfully.

An article, - very complimentary - which appeared in the Manchester Chronicle about this time concluded with the following note: "There is in preparation a new sketch by the Karno company. It is to be on an idea not previously exploited and will be ready for production in about five weeks. As Mr. Fred Kitchen is to play the chief part it may already be counted a success."

The new sketch was to prove yet another winner. It was "The Bailiff" which I had written in collaboration with Leonard Durrell. It was in this sketch I introduced a phrase which, I have often been told, went round the world – "Meredith, we're in."

But in the meantime I had suffered an irreparable loss in the death of my brother Richard.

For about a year Dick had been playing my old part of Sergeant Lightning with one of the Karno companies, and it was while he was at Falkirk that he came down to Glasgow to our matinee.

A curious fact was that he refused to go in front and see the show. He came behind and stood at the side of the stage all the time I was playing, but when I left he followed me to the dressing room and stayed with me there.

"Why don't you go and see the pantomime, Dick?" I asked him.

"No, I don't want to see it, Fred, I've only come down to see you."

This seemed so strange in one so closely connected with the theatre - for who of us ever goes into a theatre without wanting to see the show? - that I thought there must be something wrong, so I suggested, "You're feeling queer, aren't you, Dick?"

"Oh, no," he said. "Only a bit of a cold."

After the matinee was over he went back to Falkirk for the night show and went on as usual, but at the end of the performance he collapsed.

It happened that he was living in a flat built over the theatre there and he was put immediately to bed. They wired me the next day that he was ill and I at once had a male nurse sent to him from Glasgow, but was unable to go there myself until Sunday, when I motored over with my wife. I stayed with him till late that night and then motored back to Glasgow.

Here a strange thing happened. We had just got to the centre of the town when the car stopped dead, and all the efforts of the chauffeur, a clever mechanic, to find out what was wrong were unsuccessful.

The clock on the car had also stopped - at midnight exactly.

My wife and I got out and walked to our digs.

At eight o'clock the following morning, the male nurse, whom I had sent to look after my brother, came over from Falkirk and told me, "Poor Dick, your brother, passed away last night at twelve o'clock!"

This was a terrible blow to me, for Dick and I had been the greatest of friends. Indeed, he had been as much a father to me as a brother, and so often had we worked together that I had come to admire him as much as to love him. He was a great artiste as well as a perfect brother, and to lose him at this age - he was only 46, in the prime of life - and I was then 32 - was the severest blow I could suffer.

How highly he was respected in the profession was shown by the sheaf of telegrams and letters of condolence my family and I received from brother artistes all over the country. In Falkirk, where he had died, during the funeral not only did practically all the shops close and the private residents lower their blinds, but even the licensed premises around the theatre closed until the funeral was over and the coaches returned. A spontaneous and wonderful tribute to a brilliant and charming man.

It was not easy to go back to Glasgow that night and play such a part as I was playing in pantomime. Indeed, I could not.

Though I went into my dressing-room and sat in my usual chair before the mirrors, I could not bring myself to make-up that night, and although my sympathetic friends advised me - and I knew they were right - that it would have been better to go on - for that is the unwritten law of our profession - my courage was not equal to it, and that one evening my understudy played for me.

Often I wonder how many people really understood how often we who amuse them have to play out in real life that "Laugh, Punchinello; for the heart is breaking;"

* * * * *

However, Time heals all wounds, and by the following night I was sufficiently the master of my feelings to resume my part, and carried on to the successful end of the show and the writing and. rehearsals of "The Bailiff."

Speaking of "The Bailiff," I must relate how that popular phrase "Meredith, we're in," originated.

Durrell and I had been busy on the script for some time, but we hadn't found a name for the bailiff's man, one of the funniest characters in the sketch.

Names, as everyone knows, are important in these things the more apt they are to the character the more simple it is to put the character over - and it had come to the morning of the day we were to open with the new show at Wigan.

We were talking it over as we walked along the street towards the theatre for rehearsal and happened to drop into the Bodega for a little refreshment on the way. There, as we stood at the bar having a drink, Durrel said to me, "Look here, Fred, we've still got to find a name for the bailiff's man. What shall we call him?"

Just at the moment I happened to look up towards a shelf over the bar and there I saw a row of Meredith & Drew's biscuit tins, with the name boldly displayed on them.

"Ah," I said, "there you are - thats a good name. Let's call him Meredith."

"Well, it's uncommon," Durrell agreed, and added, "I once knew an old chap who used to knock about Chancery Lane; he looked to me as if he might have been a solicitor struck off the rolls and might easily have been the original of the part - and his name was Meredith!"

So we called the character Meredith, and the phrase I used throughout the sketch, "We're in, Meredith" or "Meredith, we're in" has since become commonplace with a meaning all its own.

Quite recently I met a man in Portsmouth whom I hadn't seen for twenty years, and to celebrate it we went in, as one does, to have a drink, when, as we stood in the bar, someone beside us happened to say, apropos of something which I've quite forgotten now, "Meredith, we're in." My friend told me then that he had been the last few years in Canada, and even there he heard it often, though no-one seemed to know when, where or how it had originated.

And that was how it all began. That night in Wigan Meredith made his first bow to the public and between us we got them giggling so they didn't stop for years.

I heard a distinguished critic say only a few weeks ago that he thought Fred Emney in "A Sister to Assist 'er" and myself in "The Bailiff" were the two funniest performances he has seen all his life.

There's a kick in adding so much gaiety to the world and we settled down to a long run, with "The Bailiff" showing promise of outdoing any of its predecessors and breaking even Karno's own records.

From March onwards we travelled the sketch about up and down the length and breadth of the country, often, at the larger cities, staying for a straight run of several weeks. At the end of the year, when Fred Karno was producing another pantomime at the Grand Theatre, Glasgow, "The Bailiff" was playing to such good houses that he hesitated to take me away.

So for "Humpty Dumpty" at Glasgow that year he booked one of the most brilliant galaxies of stars I have seen in a pantomime. For instance, there was Clarice Mayne and "That" ("That" was Jimmie Tate, later the partner of Julian Wylie), Ernie Rees, Ernie Mayne, Jack and Evelyn, Fred Carey, and Mabel Green. Also there were Tennyson and Wallace, and Sam Poluski Junior, Charles Delph and again Kirby's Flying Ballet.

However, it seemed that I was fated not to miss the pantomime season, after all, for somehow Karno wasn't satisfied with results. Nothing but packed houses was good enough for him, and Glasgow didn't seem to take too kindly to "Humpty Dumpty."

The show had perhaps been running five weeks when one day Karno came to me when "The Bailiff" was in London and said, "Fred, I want you to go to Glasgow. What the show needs up there is a good dame part like you did last year."

"But I can't," I said. "Look how we're booked up with 'The Bailiff' - and, anyway, there isn't a part for me in 'Humpty Dumpty'."

But it was no good arguing, "You can write a part," he said.

Write a part I did, and off to Glasgow with it I went. And we worked out a spectacular comic entrance and a lot of new gags and I joined the cast. And I hope I shall not be accused of undue modesty when I mention that I must have struck just the lucky line the Glaswegians liked, for the takings bucked up and the show from then on went over even to Karno's satisfaction.

But I was rather glad when it was over, for my heart was really with Karno's sketches rather than his pantomimes, and I went cheerfully back to take up my part again in "The Bailiff" and later to another sketch which, if it is not so well remembered, was, I think personally, just as funny.

This was "Perkins, M.P." which was the last of the long series of sketches which I had worked in with Fred Karno, and since the history of it is very much on a parallel with that of its predecessors there is little point in enlarging upon it.

But since it was the sketch which concluded a happy association that had lasted for nearly ten years and had brought me a personal reputation which altered my whole life and career, I cannot close this chapter without quoting from an Illuminated Address presented to me by the members of the company when we parted finally on January 22nd, January 1910.

I still count the Address as one of my most precious possessions. It reads:

AN ADDRESS

to

FRED KITCHEN ESQ:

From the Members of

FRED KARNO'S PERKINS, M.P. CO.

We, the undersigned, as a token of sincere esteem and loyal affection beg to show this form of appreciation on the occasion of your leaving the Boys and Girls of Fred

Karno's Company with whom you have been so long associated.

The tribute we would strive to pay you as a Great Comedian and greater comrade cannot be expressed in words, though in our hearts we deplore your loss, a void which nothing can fill. Our sincere and assured wish is that success upon success will ever be your portion through life, which will be watched with keen devotion and admiration by all those who love and honour you.

    In bidding you Au Revoir with full hearts,
        We remains,
            Ever yours sincerely,

Aggie Morris	Lou Benjamin	Fred Carrington
Vera Gilda	Tim McDonough	Harry H. Reeves
Hermance Kitchen	Jack Osborne	Sam Poluski Junr.
Alma May	Joe Chamberlain	Ted B. Almonte
Evie Carrington	W. Farquharson	W. Powell
Laura Fletch	W. Walford	George Richards
Little Dorrit	Bert Wallace	Albert Bruno.
Florence R. Nelson	Herbert Sidney	
Tom Nelson	Phil Sinclair	

    January 22nd, 1910.
    Truly a happy ending to a very happy period.

Chapter XVI

I left Fred Karno for the purpose of joining forces with another good showman and brilliant producer, Herbert Darnley, who was planning to form a new company to tour with comic sketches.

I had known Darnley more or less all my life. First I became acquainted with him as a member of the McCarthy family, of whom there were several members, clever all-round performers.

Then I knew him as one of the Brothers Darnley who did an excellent comedy double act, and it was while they were performing under this name that Herbert was writing songs for Dan Leno. He did, I believe, write most of Leno's greatest successes.

A year or two before I left Karno the Brothers Darnley had dissolved their partnership and Herbert was producing sketches on his own, and already had with him two of Karno's old boys, Billy Reeves, the original "drunken swell" in "Mumming Birds" and Charlie Bell, the original "cheeky boy in the box."

He was now proposing to put a second company on the road and made me a very good offer to co-operate with him in writing suitable sketches and, of course, to star in them. So we settled down to work immediately and "Private Potts" was born, and after a fortnight's rehearsal we opened at the Holborn and Kilburn Empires - which meant pretty hard work from the kick-off, for it was four shows a night and widely separated at that.

With me in the company were little Harry Lappo, who had come over with me from the Karno Company, and Jack Williams, who was making his first appearance as a juvenile lead, and who later, after the death of his cousin Fred Emney took over the famous part of "Mrs. May" in "A Sister to Assist 'Er." Incidentally, I should mention that Jack Williams, after my three-years contract with Darnley was ended, took over my old parts in the "Private Potts" series of sketches, and proved himself a really first-class comedian. To-day I count him among my best friends as I did his father, Arthur Williams (the uncle of Fred Emney).

This "Private Potts" came into existence and immediately took a place in the hearts of the music-hall public. During the next three years "Potts" came to be as well-known as any of my previous characters, and he was a versatile fellow. Successively he became "Private Potts," "Persevering Potts" and "Potts in Port." And wherever he went he got a vociferous welcome.

Soon after starting with Darnley an old friend of mine, Joe Burgess, came to see me and I introduced him to Herbert Darnley.

I had known Joe for many years. I met him the first time way back at the Grand Theatre, Islington, in that disastrous pantomime when the theatre was burned down after we had played for only a fortnight. He had played with me, too, in the Karno company.

A remarkable character was Joe, as well as a very clever comedian. As a young man he had travelled with a well-known producer named Joe Eldred, a gentleman whose greatest interest was devoted to racing - to such an extent that he was able to bring a racing interest into his theatrical productions, which was, to say the least of it, ingenious.

In one of his shows there was a court scene which included a jury, and Joe, who knew everybody in the racing world, would nightly collect as many of his jockey friends as possible to sit in the box as jurymen. Such famous lights as Fred Archer, George Fordham and most of the leading jockeys of Fred Archer's time all came along to support their friend Joe Eldred.

It was naturally a great attraction and I have no doubt a similar sort of thing would be today. I imagine that the possibility of seeing Gordon Richards, Steve Donoghue, Fred Fox and Joe Childs and the rest, all acting as supers on the stage for the fun of the thing would fill any theatre to overflowing any evening!

Joe Eldred was one of those gentlemen who was quite often sought by people who had documents which they were specially desirous of presenting to him in person. In most towns someone would be lying in wait to catch him unsuspectingly with writ or summons or to seize his person.

But Eldred was equal to them. Whatever theatre he was at, there his scouts were placed about it and it only needed a suspicious character to appear anywhere on the horizon for Joe to be informed.

Joe Eldred would then send for Joe Burgess. Whereupon Burgess would put on Eldred's make-up and finish the performance for him and play for the rest of the week. And no more was seen of Joe Eldred that week...

Many a time Joe Burgess has been arrested for Eldred, but they couldn't keep the wrong man inside.

My introduction of Joe Burgess to Darnley was sufficient to get Joe instated in the company and he played with us for a long time - until, in fact, one unfortunate night soon after our opening with "Potts in Port".

We were playing the Empire, Stratford, and on that particular night Mr. Darnley had brought down Mr. Frank Allen, then chairman of Moss Empires Ltd., to see the production.

Everything went very nicely until Joe's entrance. Joe was playing the harbour-master.

Joe that day had been out with a few friends, and somehow had become a little unsteady in his gait; but even that might not have been noticed if, as he made his entrance across the rostrum, he had not swerved just a little too far over and - fallen into the "harbour."

We got through the show somehow without him, but it was too much to be overlooked and the moment the first house was over Darnley came round to the dressing-room and paid poor Joe off there and then.

That, however, was not the end of it.

I was sitting in my room waiting for the second house that night when there was a tap on the door and Joe entered.

I was still upset about what had happened, because I had been to a good deal of trouble to persuade Herbert to engage Joe, and when I saw him come in I felt I was entitled to say something about it.

He came into the middle of the room, shame-faced, apologetic, humble.

"Joe," I said, as he stood there silently, "I am surprised at you - letting me down like that, old man. You promised me you'd be good, and then the very first night that Darnley comes in and brings Mr. Frank Allen with him you go and mess everything up....."

Poor Joe stood there, crestfallen and contrite, but not a word.

"You know, it's not you that gets the blame," I went on - and I'm afraid I was working myself up just to turn the knife in the wound - "you know it's not you that gets the blame so much as me, because I introduced you... and what hurts me most is your getting the sack for having too much to drink."

Joe still stood there mum, a funny expression on his face (and he had a funny expression) and said never a word.

I said, "Joe! After all your years on the stage, I'm surprised at you. You! Getting the sack for being boozed! Haven't you anything to say?"

"Yes," he muttered at last.

"Well, what?"

"Well," said Joe, as if it explained everything, "it isn't the first time."

That dried me up, and Joe went away and I saw nothing of him for some weeks.

The next time he appeared we were still playing "Potts in Port," that week at the Coliseum, London. When I went to the theatre on the Monday morning I found Joe waiting for me and he said, "Fred, I'm not doing anything. Things are pretty bad. Do put me in."

"But, Joe," I replied, "how can I? After what happened. It's impossible.

"Well," he said, "I hear that the supers are getting a guinea. Let me go on in the crowd."

I pointed out the difficulty. "Suppose Darnley were to notice you?" I said, "Then all the old trouble would be dragged up and start all over again - and we'd both be for it!"

Joe had an idea.

"I've got a crepe hair beard I could put on; he'd never know me in that."

So I gave in. You couldn't resist Joe for long. I spoke to the super-master and Joe was put in, crepe beard and all.

Everything went well until the matinee performance on Wednesday, when the super-master came and told me that Joe hadn't turned up.

"Don't take any notice," I said, "perhaps he'll be in to-night."

But at night there was still no sign of Joe.

After the performance, I dropped in, as was my habit, to the little saloon bar two or three doors away from the stage door of the Coliseum. As I was sitting there taking a little nightcap before going home, a banjo began to twang in the passage, and a voice I recognised as that of our missing Joe Burgess began a song that went something like this:

"We had to carry Barry to the boathouse,
We had to carry Barry to the shore,
And why we carried Barry to the boathouse – was
He'd won it as he'd won it once before!"

Which referred to the fact that Barry, that great sculler, had that day again succeeded in winning the World's Sculling Championship, on the Thames.

Joe Burgess, the modern troubadour, had written a few verses and chorus and coaxed some little printer way down Camberwell way to print him off a few copies! Then, borrowing a banjo, he had set out for an afternoon's entertainment and profit-making on the towpath.

By the time he came into the bar I was ready for him - but it was no use. You couldn't be angry with Joe. His very first words disarmed me.

"Oh, don't be cross, Fred," he said as he saw me. "I won't charge you for the Monday and Tuesday I played. But I thought I'd get more than a guinea with the old banjo and the song I had written!"

He certainly had, for he had pockets full of coppers, threepenny-bits and sixpences.

"But when did you write the song?" I asked him.

"Yesterday."

"But the race wasn't held until today. What if Barry hadn't won? What would have happened to your copies then?"

"Well," said Joe ingenuously, "if he had been beaten I could have been back for the night performance and I should only have missed the matinee!"

Just one more story of Joe.

It was years later, when I was running my own shows. I was playing at the Palace Manchester, and as was my custom then I had been to London for the week-end.

On the Monday evening I arrived in Manchester and went straight to the Palace, got myself made up and went down to the side of the stage - and whom should I see there but Joe, made up and standing in the wing.

"Hello, Joe!" I said. "What are you doing here?"

"Working," he replied.

"Working? Who are you working with?"

"I'm with you," he said, with that innocent guile of his which was calculated to soften the heart of a stone.

"What d'you mean - with me?" I demanded.

"Well, I came round to see you this morning, but you were in London, so I saw your wardrobe mistress and told her to give me some props - and here I am, ready to go on."

"But," I resisted feebly, "you don't know anything about the show."

"That's all right," he replied, "I'll make one more in the crowd. I must have a couple of pounds at the end of the week because the landlady's been worrying me."

He won, as he was bound to do, and on the Saturday night I gave him two pounds ten and wished him goodbye and good luck and off I went to London on the midnight train as usual.

The following week I was opening at Nottingham, and when on Monday evening I arrived at the side of the stage there was Joe again, made up and ready to go on.

I said, "Hello, Joe", what are you doing here this time? (Though I knew well enough, and had capitulated in advance).

He said, "I'm still with you."

"Well," I asked hopelessly, "how long are you with me for?"

"As long as this tour lasts!"

Now, I ask you. Can you tell a man like that off?

* * * * *

This story is intended rather to be a chronicle of my stage career than a narrative of family life, but it is perhaps not inappropriate here to devote a few lines to tell of some of those little personal matters that, just as with every father, interested and influenced me in everything that I did from now on.

I had become very much a family man. My son Fred, whom I have referred to earlier and who is now following enthusiastically and, I am glad to say, successfully in his father's footsteps, was now beginning to grow up and was at school at Abingdon near Oxford. His two elder sisters, Cossie and Gladys, were there also. There was another girl, Nellie, and in April 1912 my fourth daughter, Joan, was born.

Fred, much to my disappointment at that time, seemed to show no inclination whatsoever for the stage, which rather surprised me. True, whenever the children were at home together and I was due home for the weekend they would rarely fail to produce some little play.

They would write the play, rehearse it, and produce it really well in the drawing-room at home.

As the girls grew up, the three youngest developed a real passion for acting, although Cossie, like her brother (the two who were really destined to have most to do with the boards) seemed to regard it with distaste.

Those Sunday night plays were rather wonderful, and I think we managed to have as merry a time as any family could ever have, for not only did the young children enjoy themselves but the old children, too.

Whenever the youngsters had warned us that they were ready to play one of their own plays for me, my wife and I would invite many of our own friends - nearly all "pros" of course - and then would be seen how the most grown-up among them, under the influence of the children's laughter, would become children themselves.

Many and many a play have we produced extempore. Two or three times, for instance, I remember we did "Aladdin" throughout. And what a cast we would have! There would be, for example, Fred Groves as the Widow Twankey, Murray Carrington as "Aladdin," Charlie Baldwin as Abanazar, my son Fred and myself as the Chinese policemen, Ben Albert, my old school-friend Frank Calvert, and at the piano my musical director, Dudley Powell.

The fun grew fast and furious, for we had no script, and no songs. It was all made up as we went along, even to the music, and I shudder to remember some of the doggerel that we turned out on the spot.

Our best audience, I think, was Jack Williams. He always came prepared. He tends towards the rotund in figure, and he would always seat himself on the lowest drawing-room chair, so that when he began to laugh, as he knew he would, he could roll off without hurting himself!

He would laugh till he cried for mercy and yelled, "Oh, turn it off! Oh, turn it off!"

One night I remember we played "The Silver King," and I said to young Fred, "Fred, you get some 'snow' and follow me about." He did, and it rather spoiled the middle of the scene when I glimpsed my wife's face in the audience and heard the guffaws of laughter that greeted the snowstorm, for Fred had gone to the kitchen and got the largest bag of flour he could find - which wasn't good for the drawing room carpet.

The 'snow' he should have used, of course, was paper cut up with scissors into tiny pieces!

But then, as every comedian knows, and it's a saying in the profession, "every laugh is worth a pound," and young Fred did at least show originality.

It was really remarkable how my good wife stood for the way we used to knock her house about, for not only was it nearly always full of happy and noisy "pros" but even when they weren't filling up every corner, the place was cluttered up with pets, for which we all had rather a weakness.

At one time, I remember, I had a huge sheep-dog, a Shetland pony, a parrot, a fighting-cock, forty-eight canaries, a cat, and what I think was the smallest Yorkshire terrier in the United Kingdom. (This last little bit of doginess weighed only fifteen ounces and I used to carry it in my breast pocket. I was offered £1,000 for it once, but declined it - and a couple of months or so later it was stolen!)

Then once I bought a donkey. We shall never forget him. He cost me thirty shillings, which I thought was not expensive - but what I didn't know was what that donkey was going to cost me.

I led him home myself, and you should have seen the children as they clambered excitedly and joyously all over Neddie. What times they saw before them - what rides!

We let him run about the lawn. That caused the first disaster. He swallowed and destroyed about thirty pounds' worth of our vegetables and flowers before we found how much he liked them.

So we decided to tie him up. I bought a tent for him and for a while all went well. Until one very stormy night. The rain was pouring down and the wind blowing a howling gale. It was a night to snuggle down in bed, but about four o'clock in the morning I was awakened by a noise that might have come from Dante's Inferno. I sat up and listened, and then distinctly I could hear the loud braying, braying, braying of Neddie. He seemed to be in torment, if the noise he was making was any indication. There was nothing for it but to get up and investigate.

I struggled outside, to discover that the tent had been blown away, and the donkey lay kicking and squirming on the ground and the tent-rope wound about his neck and nearly strangling him. I rescued him just in time.

Next morning we decided that he must have a more substantial dwelling-place. So there and then I went to a builder and he erected a small stable. Three days after Neddie had taken up his residence there I had a call from the district surveyor.

Did I have authority to build this stable? Had the local authorities granted me permission?

Of course they hadn't. I had never asked them! Very well, I had broken the law. The stable must be pulled down at once. And it was.

Then I sent Neddie to lodge with a local corn-merchant who charged me £1 a month for lodgings. He was there for three years, and I only saw him twice during all that time I reckoned he had cost me £200, and thought it was about time to get rid of him. I did. I sold him for thirty shillings - the price I had originally paid for him.

Yes, donkeys are expensive pets. Perhaps little Fred was right when he said, "Well, Daddy, you should have bought a racehorse!"

Suppose I had kept that donkey, and he had lived as long as the famous donkey owned by Jack Buer, a popular circus clown whom I knew well! His donkey, which was called Domino, was generally supposed to be ninety years old! Buer himself had had him more than fifty years. I saw a good deal of Jack Buer the time he broke in a dog for me which I used in "Private Potts." Buer lived on the Prince of Wales's estate at Kennington, and many times the young Prince paid him surprise visits.

Buer was very proud of a signed photograph the Prince had given him and had it on the wall together with a picture of George Robey, one of the famous Domino the donkey, and one of myself, and he told me once that one day when the Prince called, he looked up at the clown's art gallery - the Prince, the comedians, and the donkey - laughed, and said, "I see you've put us all together, Mr. Buer!"

Another day he called with the Queen, and introducing Her Majesty, said simply, "Mr. Buer, I've brought Mother to see you."

A Press photographer who happened to be near the Royal party was permitted to take a photograph of the three together, and Buer proudly gave me a copy later. He regarded it as one of his most treasured possessions until the day he died.

Chapter XVII

Not least among the changes I have seen during my sixty years of stage life has been that in the attitude both of public and trainer towards performing animals.

Time was when the feelings or hurts of an animal were the very last consideration, so long as it could be taught somehow to perform its tricks, but today, and indeed for the last twenty or thirty years I doubt if there has been a single case of serious cruelty in this country in training any sort of animal for the stage.

It was the same at one time with children. Not that there was always cruelty, but there was certainly a good deal of it; but I remember that even my father, in his day, used to say that if one could not train a child or an animal without being cruel, it would never make a good performer.

The vigilance of the R.S.P.C.A. has had a very considerable effect, also, apart from the general development of a higher feeling of humanity and an ever-increasing hatred of cruelty. In my earlier days I saw some acts of cruelty towards animals on the stage and was disgusted and saddened by them, but latterly - for the last twenty or thirty years - I do not recall a single case. I have always made a point of watching the rehearsals of animal acts that have been on a bill with me and so have probably had more opportunity than most to observe the kindness with which trainers treat their animal performers.

Animal acts have ever had something of a fascination for me, for, as the reader will have gathered, I am one of those people with a genuine love for our four-footed friends. I have played on the stage with them so many, many times, and have used them often in my own productions.

In my childhood days animals were even more popular on the stage than they are today. I have mentioned the pantomime I played in when I was about seven years old in which there was a scene peopled by live animals of all sorts - including a cow from my mother's ginger-beer and milk kiosk in St. James's Park. Another of my earliest recollections is of one of those dog dramas which were something of a rage sixty or seventy years ago. These dramas were written entirely around the "personality" of a dog, and it was the dog which was the real "hero" of the play.

Often I have heard. my father tell a story of when he and my uncle, Tom Lamb, travelled a dog - or rather, two dogs, for even a dog, playing so important a part as it played in these dramas, had to have an "understudy" - in a dog drama called "The Forest of Bonde."

The story concerns a time when they were to play at Dublin. Neither of them had been there before, but when they arrived with their two huge Newfoundland dogs, the Irish porters gathered about the dock immediately recognised them from the posters that had been displayed for days all over the town.

"Well, and it's dear Mr. Lamb and Mr. Kitchen," and "Well, sure an' ye're lookin' as well as ever," and such like blarney greeted the two as the porters swarmed around them. "We'll see to your baggage for ye, bless yer hearts," and one or two of them began to gather up the props.

"Here, put those things down," cried Lamb, none too politely, and in about two seconds there was a first class argument on, and in a few more it had become so heated that Lamb said to father, "Here, Dick, take the dog. I'll damn soon show these blokes!"

And no doubt he would, for he was the same Tom Lamb who could fell a bullock with a blow of his fist, and the moment my father took over the dog he sailed into the crowd of porters with a whoop of joy.

It might have been a pretty scrap, too, except that the Irishmen got an ally from a most unexpected source. It happened that in the play there was a thrilling fight scene. The dogs had been trained to dash into the middle of the fight and seize the villain of the piece (my uncle) by the throat. So, seeing him sail into the battle, no doubt they thought it was merely another rehearsal, and, knowing their part so well, they dashed out of my father's hold and went for poor Tom in good style! By the time father had pulled them off, it was Tom Lamb who had received the hiding, not the porters!

Another dog my father had was one called Kilroy, which he hired out to act in a production of "The Wandering Jew" at the Adelphi Theatre. Kilroy was trained to follow at the heels of the Jew throughout the play, but I remember him principally for the way his name was used to advertise the show.

At dawn on the morning of the opening performance a large number of men were sent out armed with huge stencils and pails of white paint and on every corner they painted on the pavements this one word, Kilroy.

The producer was summoned and fined, but it seems to have put both the production and the dog on the theatrical map.

A good many people today will remember Woodward's performing seals. I remember Mr. Woodward's father when I was a boy; he used the large bath at the Royal Aquarium which was afterwards taken by the Beckwith family for their famous swimming displays, and the Woodward of the later generation took part in the performance with his little sister. They were towed round the bath by one of the seals.

When young Woodward grew up and took over his father's show he developed an outlook which, to say the least of it, was rather unusual in our profession. He became an ardent Christian propagandist, and one of his habits was to distribute among his brother pros marked copies of the New Testament.

Many a time on a Saturday night when artistes, who had been playing together for the week would be saying good-bye, or at times when performers might be taking a drink between the first and second houses at night, he would join the party and solemnly hand each man a New Testament.

He never "preached" or interfered with other people's amusement or entertainment in any way, and his gift was always accepted gratefully and seriously. Everyone, I think, liked him and thought a great deal of him, besides admiring him for his obvious sincerity.

Birds have had their place on the stage, too, and when I was about eight years old a popular turn of the time was Petro Carl and his performing pigeons.

Petro used to keep his pigeons in a back kitchen of the house where my father and mother lived in Oakley Street, and one day I was responsible for an "accident" that very nearly ruined his act.

I threw a stone through the kitchen window!

And out flew the pigeons.

When poor Petro came that evening to collect his birds for the show - no birds! They were cooing down at him from the neighbouring roofs.

He coaxed them down in time, but it gave him a very anxious half hour.

Petro used to drive from music hall to music hall in a little trap with the pigeons in baskets at the back. Often I went with him, but not, as you might suppose, to mind the pigeons or take any part in the show - but to sit in front and start the applause after every trick!

Mentioning Petro Carl reminds me of a little story which, though it has nothing to do with animals, is so unusual that I must tell it.

Carl hired his trap from a man named Tom Hood, who drove it for him. Tom owned a little shop in Oakley Street where he sold ginger-beer, and he was the champion "bottle-carrier" of his time. Nature itself seemed to have designed him to attain this high honour.

In the championship contest each man had to carry a 4-gallon bottle upside-down on his head, and through carrying the bottle so much, on top of Tom's cranium there had developed a bump which just fitted into the neck of the bottle as though it was a stopper!

Tom must have been a man of very considerable powers of endurance for I remember that he walked from London to Brighton balancing one of these bottles.

Another popular bird-turn which a good many present-day people will remember was Marvelle and his performing cockatoos. Marvelle's real name was Jack Adby.

There must have been nearly as many different sorts of animals exploited on the stage as there are in the Zoo. My old friend Nat Emmett, whom I have mentioned earlier, when he played in "Valentine and Orson" had a real bear which had an important role in the play.

Emmett also played Dick Turpin and had a splendid mare for Black Bess. I must tell you a story of a trick played on poor old Nat.

In "Dick Turpin" one scene depicted the outside of an old inn - table and stool in the foreground and all that. Dick would ride dashingly on to the stage.

"Ho, there! Within, there! Host!"

Enter Landlord. Turpin orders a drink. The landlord brings it and then stands making a great fuss of Turpin and admiring bonny Black Bess.

"Bless her heart," says Turpin, "she knows every word I say. She'll do anything for me."

Then he takes his lace handkerchief, walks to centre of stage, drops the kerchief on the ground and then, returning to the table, seats himself and says to the mare, "Bess, my handkerchief."

Then the beautifully trained animal would trot majestically across the stage, pick up the dainty little piece of cambric, and bring it gracefully to her master's hand.

One night it had come to the moment when this pretty little act was being done. Nat Emmett had said, "Bess, my handkerchief," and Bess obediently had crossed to where it lay, put down her lovely head, but, instead of touching it, sniffed and shuddered and whinnied miserable - and left the handkerchief where it lay.

Surprised, Nat cried, "Why, what ails the mare?" and again, "Bess, my handkerchief."

Again the animal essayed to obey him, only to shudder and back nervously away.

Emmett, surmising now that something must be very wrong indeed, himself walked over and picked up the little square. He held it to his nose, frowned and then, turning to the audience, he said, "Ladies and gentlemen, please don't blame Bess. It wasn't her fault. Some evil-minded scoundrel in the company has saturated the handkerchief with paraffin oil!"

Then later came Leoni Clarke's performing cats, rats and mice - all mixed up together! And the famous Lockhart's elephants. Everyone will remember the tragic accident which happened to poor Lockhart, a great showman and a very delightful man, who, just as he had sold his elephants and was about to retire, was crushed by one of the animals and killed.

I remember a curious incident that occurred in connection with Lockhart's elephants. I was playing with Charles Lauri at the Paragon in the Mile End Road at the time.

The whole Lauri troupe had just entered through the big scenery entrance at the side of the stage door when suddenly a tremendous clamour broke out and somebody shouted "Quick - get up against the wall!"

We all rushed for the wall, and only just in time, for in a moment, trumpeting wildly, the whole troupe of maddened elephants, their trunks thrust high in the air, and creating such a terrifying racket as I have never heard elsewhere, came stampeding out, and would certainly have crushed a good many of us to death had we been in their way.

All because during the performance a mouse had run across the stage!

Speaking of elephants reminds me too of a remarkable incident in connection with Lord George Sanger's Circus. It is generally believed that "an elephant never forgets" and whether this is the fact or not, this incident certainly seems to bear out the theory.

Sanger had discovered that one of his tent-men had been behaving cruelly to one of the elephants, and he discharged him. Some ten years or so later, long after this had been forgotten, a new man who had just been taken on by Sanger was picked up by one of the animals, dashed to the ground, and trampled to death.

Then it was discovered that it was the same man who had previously been fired for cruelty.

In contrast to performing elephants another turn that was popular was Niblo's talking parrots - a wonderful turn in which the birds spoke two or three different languages and would infallibly reply to questions put to them. This I have always thought was marvellous, considering that they had to do it all twice nightly.

French poodles were very common on the stage years ago. A very clever poodle I remember came over from Germany with a man called Herr Tholen. This was a singing poodle. The dog would sit on a stool and sing up and down the scale – from high notes to low and from low notes to high, to the accompaniment of a clarinet.

When I was in Marseilles I met a friend who had a poodle which seemed almost human.

We might be sitting outside a café on one of the boulevards and if my French friend required anything he simply spoke to the dog and said, "fetch me this," or "fetch me that," and the dog did it. For instance, if he desired tobacco, he would wrap the necessary money in a piece of paper, give it to the poodle and say, "tabac," and away would go the animal, to return a minute later with tobacco. Or he would wrap up a coin and say, "journal," and back would come the dog with a newspaper.

Sometimes late at night, if he happened to have forgotten his key, he would merely ask the dog to fetch it, and sure enough in due course the poodle would return with the missing key.

The extraordinary devotion of this dog to his master was such that when the man died and the funeral was about to start for the cemetery, the dog had to be shut in an upstairs room to prevent it following its masters coffin to the grave. However no-one noticed that the window of the room was open, and, at the moment when the hearse was moving off, the poodle jumped to its death on the pavement below.

I have told about Charles Lauri and what a wonderful animal impersonator he was. His impersonation of Sally, the Zoo chimpanzee, has never been equalled and he was one of the best "cats" that ever appeared in pantomime. Another clever pantomime "cat" was Fred Whittaker, who played the cat in Karno's production "The House that Jack Built" in Glasgow.

A few months before the start of this pantomime, when I was talking it over with Karno, I suggested to him that it might be a good idea if we got some real cats for the scene in which I had to come on and say "Puss, puss," and pour out a saucer of milk which Freddy had to lap up. My idea was that we should have, say, a dozen real cats to follow Freddy on and give me a chance to crack a gag such as, "My word, what a family - and I never even knew that he was married!"

Karno agreed that it was a good idea, and asked a man who used to hang about Brixton to find him a dozen stray cats. One day the fellow was shown into the office in Vaughan Road, Camberwell, with two sacks - six cats in each sack!

"Well, how much?" asked Karno.

"Three pounds, guv'nor."

"What! Three pounds for stray cats," Karno expostulated. "It's a lot."

"Well, take 'em or leave 'em," said the man. "If you don't want 'em I'll let 'em loose in the office."

Karno took them.

But there were still six weeks to go, and the problem now was what to do with them in the meantime. Fred Whittaker was away on tour, so Karno said, "Well, he's got to use them, so he'd better train them. Send them to him."

So some special little boxes were made and the cats sent off to poor Freddy Whittaker - the most remarkable and dilapidated assortment of cats that ever were seen. Some had one ear, one of them had only one eye, and they all showed signs of many gory battles - real old London scrappers they were. Whittaker had to travel these beasts from town to town for six weeks before finally he got to Glasgow, and the tales he had to tell about them when he got there. What the stage-managers had said! What the landladies had thought!

Cats like that don't take very kindly to training, either. Neither milk nor meat would persuade those wretched animals to follow Freddy across the stage so much as a yard. So in despair at last it was suggested that we should have little collars made for them, and that these collars should be attached by some thin, strong, invisible whipcord to a special collar which Freddy would wear as the stage cat. And the collars in due course arrived, in time for the dress rehearsal.

I laugh now whenever I recall the ludicrous appearance of Freddy Whittaker, sitting there in the wings in his cat's make-up with these twelve live cats scratching and mewing and howling and getting all tangled up around him.

Then came the moment when I made my entrance with a saucer of milk and called, "Puss, puss." Cue for Freddy.

Well, Freddy did his best. He tried to enter with cats, but before he'd got a yard on to the stage, what with the footlights, and the limelights, and a crash from the orchestra, demons entered into the souls of those poor, miserable, frightened animals. Pandemonium broke out. In about a second it looked like twelve dozen cats. Some broke loose and dashed with enormous leaps over stalls and pit and away into the distance; some got tied up in the whipcord and nearly strangled themselves; and altogether it was the finest cat performance that ever I saw.

We never tried live cats on the stage anymore!

Chapter XVIII

Some months before my three years' contract with Herbert Darnley was due to expire, I had decided that I would not take advantage of his offer to renew it for a further three years, but would now at last do something which I suppose every successful actor or comedian has some sort of hankering to do.

I would run my own shows.

That did not prevent me dropping a quiet word here and there where I knew it would spread and bear fruit; and it was not long before it began to be known in the places where they talk about these things that "Fred Kitchen was leaving Darnley next February."

I had expected some interest to be shown in certain places, certainly, but I must confess that I was surprised as well as delighted and flattered at the response on the part of eminent producers and impresarios.

Offers seemed to come from everywhere; and, what was best about it, most of them were good offers and tempting offers, too. I began to think that the world of professional comicality was really at my feet, and perhaps it was. None of the offers that came my way, however, pleased and flattered me so much as one which came from Mr. George Edwardes.

He offered me the position of principal comedian at the Gaiety Theatre, to take the place of Edmund Payne.

The salary, though high, did not line up with what I expected to make once I had my own productions on the road, but sometimes I think, with regret, that although, indeed, I did make a great deal more money on my own, I might have been wise to accept his offer. For I do not think there is a higher rank or a higher honour in our profession than to have been with George Edwardes. That we should have got on well together, I know; for that matter we always did. For he was a fine fellow in every way; and his shows represented the peak of popularity and public respect.

But, as I say, the cash side of it influenced me, and finally confirmed me in my decision to essay my own enterprises, and test my belief in my ability to put up the finest shows the British public had yet seen on the variety stage. I had for so many years been connected with comedy productions and had observed so often just how each type of them was received by the public, that I earnestly believed that I could put up the best shows yet; and that my reward would be in proportion.

I began to make arrangements.

To begin with I called on my old friend and collaborator, Charles Baldwin, once more and between us we wrote "Bungle's Luck", a new sketch on musical comedy lines.

I planned to produce the show in the most elaborate way. Everything was to be of the best. For my scenery I went to R.C.McCleary, a celebrated scenic painter at Drury Lane; and when it came to costumes I spared no expense. Even the clothes of messenger boys and the like in the cast were tailor made by my old friend Tom Parry, who still makes the clothes for a good many pros in his shop at New Cross. The ladies' frocks came from Swan and Edgar. It was to be the finest show that had ever seen the footlights of the music hall stage, and the cast was as large as had ever been booked for a music hall production. It included in all about sixty people.

It was a distinguished cast. Among the lady members I had Aggie Morris who had now been with me for some twelve years. There was Kate Forster, from the D'Oyly Carte company; Victor Stevens, an old Drury Lane comedian; Elmore Frith, son of the eminent R.A. whose pictures "Derby Day" and "The Railway Station" are, of course, famous; Harry Piddock, son of Charles of "The Lady Slavey" fame; J.E. Coyle, son of Johnny Coyle, the well-known comedian; Charles Baldwin; John Osborne, who had been my late brother Dick's partner; and, of course, our old friend, Harry Lappo.

In due course we went into rehearsal and the time came to "try it on the dog", by giving it a chance to break itself in with a week's run somewhere in the provinces quietly, as is the custom with new shows. I had been lucky enough to secure a three years' contract with Moss Empires Ltd. so had no worries as to where we were going or whether we could pull it off, but all the same, I felt that we should put it on quietly somewhere before coming out in an official opening in London.

We had arranged for our London debut at the Victoria Palace, London, on March 10th., when the Moss contract began; and for two weeks before this - February 24th. and March 3rd. I booked a week each at the Bedminster Hippodrome and the Palace, Plymouth, respectively.

Now I had a new and totally unexpected cause for self-congratulation in the way my friends rallied round me.

So as not to prejudice the London opening at the Victoria Palace I had done my best to keep the Bedminster and Plymouth arrangements really quiet; but in spite of all my caution the news leaked out that on February 24th. "Bungle's Luck" would make its debut.

Phil Ray, the comedian, was the first to arrive, having motored down from London to wish me luck in person; Jimmy Driscoll, the boxer and one of my oldest friends, came over from Cardiff to give me a send-off and remained with me a week; and my old sporting friend, Edward Durling, Senr. came all the way from Monte Carlo to be present at the opening night. A flood of telegrams from friends and fellow-pros all over the world wishing me and the company luck.

"Bungle's Luck" went over well, and public and Press were enthusiastic. The papers made a good deal of the elaborateness of the production and went out with a remarkable agreement for the statement that "for 'Bungle's Luck' Fred Kitchen travels a company about twenty stronger than George Edwardes employs for 'The Count of Luxembourg'." I suspect they copied it from each other!

Then, confident that we had "the goods", we came to London. I never dreamed I had so many friends! We must have given the local Post Office the shock of its life, for, from the afternoon until night, telegrams poured in from every corner of London and the country. After a while messenger boys were bringing them along in batches of fifty at a time; And before the show was over my dressing room was literally "snowed under." The familiar buff envelopes and their friendly messages lay about in stacks several feet high, and when afterwards we came to count them I found that there were more than eight hundred of these very pleasant and friendly tokens of goodwill.

Again the Press was kind. Some of the reviews, in fact, in otherwise quite sober papers, almost bring a blush to my cheek now when I re-read them. One and all the critics welcomed the new sketch and prophesied a long and successful run. It was Chance Newton, I think, who printed the only little criticism I received when he said at the end of an otherwise laudatory article in the "Referee": -

"Two things are needed for the comical Kitchen. One is a comical tag instead of the present tame musical finish; the other is less hideous make-up. It made me think that Frederick the Funny had put on a pantomime mask!"

That make-up, as a matter of fact, rather worried me, too. I would have liked to play Bungle in a much straighter make-up, but no one would hear of it. No, they all said, you must be "Kitchen."

Chance Newton was a critic for whom I had always a very high respect. There was a time when, in the "Referee" he said, "Young Fred is overdoing his whistle." This was when I was working with five of my front teeth out, and during the dialogue at about every five or six words I would emit a comical whistle, as toothless people will, and I had got so much into the habit of it that I really did it unconsciously.

One Sunday a few weeks after this note had appeared, I happened to meet Mr. Newton at Edward Cranston's house at Margate, where we were both guests.

As we sat in the garden together and talked I mentioned his criticism of me and my whistle.

I said, "You haven't heard my whistle today, have you?"

"No," he replied.

"Now," I said, "I will talk to you for a while with my teeth out."

Then he discovered that I really did not know whether I was whistling or not, and he explained it all away in his paper the following week.

This whole business of make-up has been a very large part of my work and for every part I played I gave the most careful thought and consideration to producing as laughable and yet as appropriate a make-up as I could devise; and there were always little mannerisms that I had developed as a sort of basis. One of them, for example, was that, comic little shuffle that has been the subject of so much controversy in connection with Charlie Chaplin and myself.

Chaplin has put the shuffle and the big shoes on ten thousand screens and once there came a time when I wanted to leave off the boots, because a younger generation said I was copying Chaplin!

Not for a moment do I wish to belittle Chaplin. I have the highest admiration for him and his work. I think he deserves all the wonderful success he has had, but the "resemblance" between our mannerisms has had its direct influence on my own career to such an extent that I am glad to take this opportunity of putting on record the precise facts.

A few years ago I was offered a first-rate contract to go to New York - I think it was the highest sum ever

Fred with his signature shoes

offered to a comedian up to that time - and I should have welcomed it with open arms, except that I felt that the Americans, particularly the younger people, all of whom had seen Charlie Chaplin so many times, would say that Fred Kitchen was "copying Chaplin." Which, though it would have been absolutely wrong, I considered would have hurt too much.

In November, 1929, an American stage paper called "Footlights" printed an article by Betty Ovsey, in which the whole business of who invented the "Chaplin" shuffle is raked up and analysed very thoroughly.

Because it represents, I think, the unbiased findings of a professional theatrical writer after all possible research and enquiry, I take the liberty of printing some extracts from this article which gives the facts fairly and accurately.

"Richard Dunn was an old comedian who played under the name of Richard Kitchen. He was famous in the eighties for his interpretation of the leading part in "The Dumb Man of Manchester." He suffered painfully from gout and rheumatism, and was helpless in bed for many years. When the old man began, to walk again his feet were wrapped in flannel rags. One foot pointed sharply to the right, the other sharply to the left. Everyone laughed. His son (Fred Kitchen) used that walk for the first time in 1903. He was starred as Sergeant Lightning in "The Dandy Thieves." The walk amused the British Isles and became associated with Kitchen.

"This is the origin of Charlie Chaplin's famous shuffle. George Dollini, whose English stage name was Gipsy Dolin, was with Chaplin for several years. He tells this story."

George Dollini was one of us in "Moses and Son." He was one of Karno's boys, as Charlie Chaplin was.

Then we get Fred Karno's opinion.

"Fred Karno says – "Miss Ovsey continues, – "that although Charlie did get the ideas for a number of his gags from Kitchen, the walk was not one of them. According to him Kitchen's walk was jumpy and rheumatic, while Chaplin's is a steady shuffle. .... But Kitchen must have given him the idea."

After this I leave it to the reader to say whether I was justified in feeling that the suggestion, - not to say accusation, - that I was "copying Chaplin" was, to put it mildly, undeserved!

Fred Karno's opinion, anyway, commands respect, when he says that "Chaplin did get the ideas for a number of his gags from Kitchen." That Miss Ovsey appreciates the fact is shown by the following two extracts from the second instalment of her series on Chaplin in which she gives her story of two of Charlie's little laughter-makers.

"It was the week before Christmas, 1905, at the Palace Theatre, Bordesley, Birmingham, Karno produced a comic revue, 'Moses and Son', with Fred Kitchen in the lead. Kitchen was the only Gentile in the cast — all the others were Jews. This was the most sensational revue in the English halls at the time.

"Kitchen, as the caretaker of the bank, is left in charge during the lunch hour. A messenger brings a telegram for 'Moses and Son.' Kitchen signs for it, opens, reads it, put it in his pocket. He rolls up the envelope between his palms, and flips it over his right shoulder with his right hand. But instead of hitting it with the heel of his right foot, he uses the left. This gag brought the house down, and was kept in the show as a standard laugh getter. Charlie Chaplin has used the same gag with a cigarette many times."

As far as it goes, the author is right about this little gag, but the real origin of it goes further back. One day when I was with the Charles Lauri troupe, Harry Ewens (whom I have mentioned several times in my story) and I were walking along a street in Newcastle-on-Tyne, when Harry noticed a crumpled piece of brown paper on the pavement. Ewens quite spontaneously did this little gag, bending down to pick up the crumpled roll with his right hand, throwing it over his right shoulder and making an imitation kick at it with the wrong foot, which was so spontaneously funny that it got a big laugh from me.

Then, years after, on the first night of "Moses and Son" I was handed the telegram. I opened it, crumpled up the envelope and suddenly remembered Harry Ewens joke in Newcastle. Without thinking I did the same thing with the crumpled envelope and to my own surprise it got a roar of laughter. Hence that gag.

The second of Charlie Chaplin's gags Miss Ovsey describes equally fully:

"In G.P.O., ('General Post Office'), a revue staged by Fred Karno in 1909, with Kitchen in the lead is found the source of another Chaplin gag.

"Kitchen, the caretaker of the post office, is left in charge while the postmaster-general is away. A well-dressed man enters and buys a two-cent stamp. He comes to Kitchen with the stamp in his right hand and a letter in his left and looks directly into Kitchen's eyes. Kitchen becomes uneasy. The man puts the stamp and the letter on his silk hat, takes out his watch with his right hand, and with his left feels Kitchen's pulse. He indicates with his own tongue that he wants Kitchen to show his. Kitchen does so. The man puts his watch back into his pocket, drops Kitchen's hand, takes the stamp up with his right hand and the letter with his left, and runs the stamp over Kitchen's tongue. He sticks the stamp on the envelope, picks up his silk hat, bows, and walks out. Kitchen, amid the roars of the audience, remains with his tongue hanging out."

Charlie Chaplin used this gag in his Essanay comedy, "The Bank."

Here is the real origin of this joke. It occurred when I was playing "G.P.O." at the Grand Theatre, Clapham.

My brother Harry, who was not connected with the Karno Company, came behind one night when I was on the stage, and to my astonishment walked on and worked this unrehearsed gag on me. Pantomimists we both were, and when he walked on he saw his opportunity, went through all the motions in mime, and, out of what was simply a joke played on me, we got a wonderful laugh.

It was so good, in fact, that I decided to keep it in the show and rehearsed one of the company in the part, so that it became a regular gag.

I do not want to seem to labour these references to Charlie Chaplin, but I feel that I might fairly correct one or two misapprehensions with regard to Charlie's connection with the Karno organisation, since Chaplin himself has held back his life story for the present.

Miss Ovsey's capable articles in "Footlights," well informed as they are, are not always right in detail.

"By this time Chaplin was under contract to Fred Karno for fifty-two weeks in the year. He was paid whether he worked or not. Once, when Chaplin's show closed for the summer, Karno sent him to Fred Kitchen. He asked him to give Charlie something to do. Kitchen was then featured in 'G.P.O.' (General Post Office). This was in August, 1909. The bit Charlie did was a howl, but he was not satisfied. He considered the part too small and walked out after the first performance at the Empire Holborn Theatre in London. Charlie felt that he was getting on well. He wanted to avoid the reputation of a 'bit' player."

The true facts here were that Karno sent Chaplin down to me - not at the Holborn Empire, but at the Palace, Leicester- with the suggestion that I should try him out in a speaking part.

I did try him out there for the week, and again the following week at the Palace, Manchester, in a little comedy part which I wrote especially for him. But Charlie's voice did not seem to carry, and at the end of the second week I sent him back to Karno in London.

It must have been about this time that an amusing incident occurred, connected with Chaplin. His elder brother, Syd Chaplin was also working for Karno at the time, his salary being about £15 a week to Charlie's £2. One day they were walking along Coldharbour Lane towards Camberwell Green, when Syd glanced at his brother's boots and said: "Aren't your boots in a fearful state, Charlie? Come along to the Green and I'll buy you a pair." Arriving at the boot shop, Syd said: "Are your socks all right?" Charlie replied: "one is." After that Syd was surely justified in being a bit annoyed when Charlie took off the wrong boot!

Charlie was always an eccentric and amusing little fellow; he would keep the company in roars of laughter in the dressing-rooms, and on Sunday morning at the railway stations, often turning up in the oddest costumes one could wear without risking arrest!

Stan Laurel, also an old Karno boy, who used to understudy for Charlie in the Karno sketches, has said:

"Charlie was the eternal worry of the manager. He was always sauntering nonchalantly in at the last moment while the wretched manager was frantically tearing his hair and eyeing his watch. Stan, too, suffered many pangs of uncertainty as to whether or not he was to be called in place of the erratic star.

"'But I never once had the chance to take Charlie's place in all the years I understudied for him,' declares Stan, 'although many times I was dressed and ready.'

" 'Charlie invariably showed up just in the nick of time, bland and unperturbed.

" 'His mind was usually a thousand, miles or so away, dwelling in some land where the rest of us poor troupers could not follow.'"

In conclusion, lest my opinion of Charlie should be misunderstood, let me say that on each occasion when Charlie has visited England, I have always been looked upon by the English Press as one of the people who might be referred to about him, and whenever I have been called on this subject I have had but one reply, and that my truthful and honest opinion - that I regard Charles Chaplin as the greatest comedy genius the screen has ever had.

Chapter XIX

When I made my three-years contract for sketches with Moss Empires, I reserved the pantomime seasons, as I had no wish to interrupt the long series of pantomimes I had played in over so many years. Consequently, at the end of 1913 I was back at the Grand Theatre, Glasgow, once more, rehearsing the role of Dame in "Babes in the Wood."

But "Bungles Luck" had been running so successfully that, although I preferred a pantomime part for myself, I saw no reason why I should take the show off provided I could find someone to take over my part. I did find him, in the person of Fred Bluett, an Australian comedian, whose style and build were not unlike my own and who therefore was well suited to take over the part. So "Bungle's Luck" carried on, and when pantomime was over I decided to form a second company, which I did, in this case taking over my old part of Bungle, so that there were now two complete companies running.

After a few months, however, I decided that it was time to put on a new show, and while my second company, with Fred Bluett, carried on with "Bungle's Luck" I started rehearsals with a new musical comedy sketch called "Pinkie," and produced it at the London Palladium in May, after which we went on tour.

Then came the war, and soon I began to lose the younger men of the company. First to go was Horace Wheatley, Junr., who was an old soldier and a reservist. The poor fellow was killed soon afterwards.

Others out of the casts of both companies went and I had to fill their places with older men. At the end of the year, by which time it had become all to obvious that the war was not coming to the quick end we had so optimistically anticipated at the beginning, I offered myself. We were playing in Birmingham that week and I was forty one, but as I went blithely along to the recruiting station I thought that if I subtracted a year or two from that rather forbidding total, I might easily squeeze into the ranks. But no; the doctor took one look at my feet. "You'll never march with feet like that," he said. "You're no good to us."

And that was that.

Before long, however, the old pro's, and such young ones as had not already gone, regardless of rank or shape or job, got together and formed what we called the "Horseferry Road Army." In all the big towns, where there were two or three theatres, the authorities would send along a sergeant to give us a spot of drill. Sometimes it would be on the stage of one of the theatres; sometimes on any old piece of waste ground that was handy. Sometimes it was good fun; but that was when the sergeant was the right sort. Sometimes it was no fun at all and I still have some poignant memories of the Swedish drill and the long route marches we would have to undergo if the Sergeant happened to be the sort of bloke who was devoid of due respect for our ancient profession!

These were the days when the gloom of war fell over the theatre world. Companies everywhere were playing to almost empty houses, and the outlook was indeed as black as it well could be. I, myself, had four companies on the road and was losing money every week. In fact, it cost me so much that after four or five months, I had to close down three of the companies, and kept on only the one I was playing in myself.

This, however, was bad judgment on my part, and bad luck, for a few weeks later the Press opened a campaign for brighter theatres. As they pointed out, the boys at the front wanted gaiety when they came home on leave; munition workers, too, needed relaxation. Gloom and stinginess were out of place. The result was that in a few weeks the public flocked back to theatres and cinemas, and instead of playing to empty seats, companies were finding every house packed. But I had lost so much money I could not put my companies out again.

A good many of the older actors and artistes became special constables. Edward Lauri, cousin of Charles Lauri, for instance, became Inspector of the specials at Bow Street. Among the specials at Brixton station were Ben Albert, Datas, S.W.Wyndham and Syd May, the mimic.

The only case Ben Albert ever got as a special was a little boy about six and a little girl about four who were lost. Ben took them along to the station and on the way bought them cakes and sweets, and entertained them at the station until he found out where they lived; then he took them home.

Whether it was just gratitude or a desire to show off on the part of the little boy, the lad developed the habit of bringing all his little boy friends along to the police station; pushing open the door of the room where the specials were waiting for their turn to go on duty and pointing proudly to Ben would say, "There 'e is; that's the pleeceman that took me 'ome."

It became a bit of a nuisance; Ben's comrades got too fond of saying, "Here you are, Ben. Here's your case again. He'll probably get you promotion before long."

So at last Ben went out one day to talk to the boy.

"Now, listen, sonny; I was very kind to your little sister and you when you were lost, wasn't I? And I don't like you coming round here every day and pushing the door open and pointing me out. Now, as I was good to you, will you do something for me?"

And before Ben could go on to ask the lad to stay away in future, he answered eagerly, "Yes, sir. I'll catch you a live frog!"

Syd May, the mimic whom I have mentioned, used to give a wonderful impersonation of Dan Leno. In fact, some of his mannerisms were very like those of the great Dan. One day he was on duty outside the Crown and Sceptre public house on Brixton Hill when a taxi drew up and a big, burly man got out who was rather the worse for liquor, and handed the taxi man a shilling.

" 'Ere, wot's this?" said the man. "It's three bob on the clock."

The hefty passenger replied. "Oh, it is, is it? Well, I've given you a shillin' and that's all you're goin' to get. Or you can have a punch on the nose if you like!"

"Oh, yes," said the taximan. "We'll see about that. Constable!"

Diminutive Syd May rolled up as officiously as his size allowed.

"What's all this?"

"I want another two bob. It's three bob on the clock, and he's given me a shillin'," the taximan explained heatedly.

Syd looked at the passenger. "Go on," he said. "Give the man two shillings and clear out of here."

"Oh, yes," the man replied truculently. "I've told him I'll give him a punch on the nose - and I'll give you one, too, if you're not careful - the pair of you." And he shaped up as though to suit the action to the word.

"Now, that's quite enough of that," said Syd. "We don't want any fighting here." And taking two shillings from his pocket he handed it to the taxi man and said, waving them grandiloquently away, "Now then, clear off, both of you. I'm having no disturbances on my beat!"

At this period of the war one or two of the boys in my company had obtained commissions. Among them was Tommy Kayne, who was stationed at Ripon.

Walking along the street one day he passed a private leaning against a lamp-post, and the private failed to salute him. The officer turned back and said, "Why didn't you salute me when I passed?"

"Salute you! What for?" said Harry Brown, the Tommy. "You were only one of Fred Kitchen's boys the same as I was!"

Another young officer who had just got his first pip up came home on leave for a few days to see his mother and father. The old man was naturally very proud of his son in officer's uniform, and one day was walking along the Edgware Road with the young lieutenant when a tommy coming the other way saluted. The officer returned the salute and the father raised his hat and said "Thank you!"

It was rather wonderful the amount of money obtained for war charities by our profession, not only through special benefit matinees but from special auctions and similar things. A huge amount was collected by George Robey in this way, and by Violet Loraine and heaps of other people connected with the music halls and theatres.

I had one very good afternoon in Glasgow myself when a big sale was being held in the meat market, the proceeds of which were to go to the Red Cross Fund, and I was asked if I would go on the platform with Lord Inverclyde and Sir Horace Cameron as one of the auctioneers.

Lord Inverclyde and Sir Horace, after taking a few hundred pounds, turned to me and said, "Mr. Kitchen, you can tell the tale better than we can. You had better take the hammer."

The first thing I put up for auction was a barrel of oranges, which I proceeded to sell at a shilling each. For a little while, they went well enough, but then customers dropped off, and there were still lots of oranges left.

So I had a bright idea. I took a sovereign from my pocket, pierced the skin of one of the oranges, pressed the coin into it, dropped it back in the barrel and had two men shake them up until it was impossible to guess which was the orange worth a pound. But it made all the difference; those oranges went like wildfire at a shilling a time.

And in Scotland, too!

Moreover, the gentleman who bought the lucky orange gave me back the sovereign to add to the Fund.

A tiny Shetland pony was then put up for sale, and a Scotsman and an Irishman started bidding against each other for possession of it. I got them up to £150, but I thought I could do better than this, so I asked permission of my fellow-auctioneers to join in the bidding, and make it a contest between England, Scotland and Ireland.

Everybody agreed and eventually I knocked the pony down to myself for £240. Afterwards I made a present of it to the Red Cross Fund and it was raffled and made a further £200 for the Fund. A real treasure of a pony!

When everything else had been sold I put up my walking stick for auction. It was a stick of which I was rather fond as it had been made from the propeller of one of our fighting planes which had helped to bring down the first German Zepp at Cuffley. It fetched the amazing sum of £47.10s. I wonder where it is now?

Altogether that day I took something over £3,000 for the Red Cross.

I was playing at Birmingham during the war when I went over to Wolverhampton to see an old uncle of mine who had fought with the 14th. Hussars in the Indian Mutiny, sixty years before. I asked his opinion of the war, and he said he was disgusted with the entire thing.

"I have written to the War Office twice," he said, "and they won't give me a gun. So I have written to my old Colonel and asked him to see what he could do for me."

The gallant old soldier was dying to get to the front, in spite of being nearly ninety years of age. His Colonel had been dead for some years, but strange to say, the son of his old Colonel was now Colonel of the Regiment, and whether through his influence or not I can't say, but my uncle, Troop Sergeant-Major Stratford, received a letter to say that he could go out recruiting, and informing him where to go for his khaki.

Khaki he refused to put on; he had still got his old regimentals, complete with pill-box hat. Wearing this, he went out and was successful in recruiting a large number of men - this, of course, being before the Derby Scheme came into being - and when the drafts went away he would march proudly at the head of them to see them off.

He remarked to me that the fighting in these days "was not fighting at all! That was fighting, the way we fought in the Indian Mutiny," he said. "Each side knew what time you started in the morning, then. Now, they burrow in like a lot of rabbits, turn handles of machine-guns, something hits you and you don't know who's done it. In my day, when the order was given to Charge, you saw the man you were going for, and if he got you, you had a chance to strike back. Now they fight miles apart and you can't even see what you're aiming at."

He was indeed a wonderful old soldier and died only a few years ago, aged a hundred and three. They gave him a splendid military funeral.

I had a good deal of experience of the air raids during the war, for, at this period, I was working in London a good deal. On one occasion I was working at the Finsbury Park Empire when we had rather a bad one. When I arrived at the stage door on the Monday night, the first person I met was Ida Barr, whom I had not seen for some time.

I asked how things were and she told me she had been having a shocking time. "I owe a month's rent at my flat," she said, and this week's work will be a Godsend. I shall be able to pay the landlord up, and if I only fix a few more weeks, things will be quite all right again."

Just at that moment there was a terrible crash, and a bomb fell right outside the stage door. "That's done it," said Ida, coolly. "There goes the rent!" But luckily it was not so bad as we thought and in spite of two or three raids that week we never missed a performance.

Another incident which I remember in connection with the air raids concerns Arthur Roberts.

Arthur was standing in the Cavour bar in Leicester Square one afternoon, when a bunch of German planes came over in one of their lightning raids and managed to get over the West End. A couple of bombs fell in Leicester Square.

Several women fainted and one of them, a girl of the Leicester Square class, collapsed just outside the Cavour entrance. Someone kindly carried her into the bar and laid her on one of the big loungers there.

A dear old gentleman standing there was in a terrible state. He ordered a large brandy and gave it to the girl as she was coming round. Just at the moment, too, another bomb fell and another fainting woman was carried in and laid down. Another brandy from the old gentleman.

It was remarkable how many brandies it required to revive the two women, but the old gentleman, all nerves and sympathy, did his duty nobly, if fussily. Seeing that they were coming to, however, he turned to Arthur, who had stood there watching the proceedings and consuming his own drink, and said anxiously, "Mr. Roberts, don't you know anything about first aid?" And Arthur quickly replied, "No, I haven't got sufficient change!"

Passing the Midland Hotel in Liverpool one day, I met two brothers named Walker, whom I knew. I was a great friend of their Uncle, who was connected with the well-known brewery firm of Walkers. Both could easily have obtained commissions had they wished, but had preferred to join as privates.

They invited me into the Midland to have a drink. We entered the bar and at the other end an officer was standing in conversation with the barmaid. She came over to us and the younger of the Walker lads had just ordered drinks when the officer called the girl back and told her to tell the two soldiers that they could not be served while there was an officer in the bar.

So back came the girl, and told us she was sorry, but that she could not serve us.

We had to leave and went to a small public house nearby, and as we left the elder Walker said to the younger Walker, "Did you know that chap?"

He replied, "Yes, he's a Walker."

"A Walker?" said the elder one in surprise, "No relation of ours, surely?"

"No," said his brother. "He is a shopwalker at Lewis's!"

Chapter XX

I have said that when war began I was playing a sketch entitled "Pinkie." It was one of the few sketches in which I ever played when I could not feel the intense enthusiasm and interest which I have always tried to put into my work. "Pinkie," so far as I could see was as funny as my other sketches, and was well praised by the critics; but playing in it left me with the unusual and unsatisfactory feeling, - "Well, thank heaven that's over."

Feeling thus, I was glad when the pantomime season came round once more and I could find in that an excuse to abandon "Pinkie" for ever. I willingly accepted an offer from Mr. Francis Laidler to play in "Cinderella" at Leeds.

Mr. Laidler, before booking the company, suggested that, in view of the less satisfactory business to be anticipated on account of the war, I should take less than I usually accepted for the company. I agreed, and was happily surprised a fortnight or so before the pantomime ended when he came to me and said: "Mr. Kitchen, you were so reasonable in accepting the 'cut' I suggested, and business has been so much better than we had dare hope, that I should like you to let me give you a special benefit night during the last week."

Shortly afterwards came Mr. Laidler's manager to tell me he had arranged for the benefit to be on the last Friday night of the run. Evidently the news had gone round before even I knew the date, for, on leaving the theatre that night I called at the Victoria Club, the rendezvous of the sporting people of Leeds, and met an old friend of mine, one George Yates, a bookmaker, who asked, "Fred, are you having a Benefit?" and when I confirmed this pleasant fact, said, "Well, book me a box and the first two rows of the stalls!" Then, turning to some of the sporting fraternity there remarked, "Boys, if you want any tickets for Fred's benefit night, you'd better put your names down now, or you won't get them."

Within half an hour nearly all the stalls, circle and dress Circle, were booked, and a day or two later every seat in the house was sold except the gallery (which was not bookable) and one private box, and this box had been reserved - and paid for - by Mr. Laidler himself - a very complimentary action, I thought, in view of the fact that he was the proprietor of the theatre.

All my friends who were appearing at other places of entertainment that week offered their services generously to play for me that night, but unfortunately permission was refused for them to appear by one of the managements. Wilkie Bard, when he found that he would not be allowed to appear, sent to me at the theatre a lovely little diamond and turquoise tie-pin accompanied by the friendliest of letters telling me how much he regretted being barred from supporting me personally and asking me to accept the pin as "a token of his regard."

Malcolm Scott was another who resented being forbidden to come along. But, ban or no ban, he came. Judge my astonishment when, halfway through the show, he turned up, made-up as Catherine Parr - a characteristic part of his - and said:

"Permission or no permission, Fred, I'm going on for you. I've known you so many years now, they've no right to stop me. Come on, we're going to have a little drink, and I'm going on."

And we had our little drink, and he went on. It was a genuine tribute which I have always appreciated. But then I have always been immensely fortunate in having so many genuine and generous friends.

To put it briefly, the night was a most successful one, and I have never seen so many presents given publicly to a performer as were handed to me at the finish of the show, with the exception of the present-day pantomimes at the Alexandra Theatre, Birmingham, of which more later. I received umbrellas, cigarette cases, cases of whisky, flowers, walking-sticks, mufflers, pocket-handkerchiefs and such a miscellaneous collection of articles as might honour a bridegroom, including another breast-pin with my initials in diamonds.

Those were the days!

It reminded me of the old days at places like the Britannia at Hoxton, and the Old Vic and Surrey Theatres, on benefit nights, when all sorts of odd presents were handed over the footlights by the admirers of the performer whose benefit it was. Legs of mutton, joints of beef, a nice large codfish, a plate of whelks, or maybe a bottle of whisky from the local publican, were not at all unusual, nor less welcome than, say, a pair of trousers from the local tailor!

Once, I remember, my father, on one of his benefit nights, got a pair of white doves.

There were certain things that were welcome at our home, and certain things that weren't, and Dad decided that doves came definitely under the latter heading. Besides, we had a cat. So he suggested to my brother Harry, who was with him then, that he should take the doves out the following day and try to sell them. That night they were left at my aunt's house - I suppose father thought that aunt was less likely to raise practical objections, or anyway might be willing to give the unwelcome strangers at least a night's hospitality; and on the morrow Harry set forth to find a buyer.

He took them into an animal shop in the Waterloo Road not far from the theatre, and asked the proprietor what he would give for them.

"Well, they aren't worth much," said the man, "but I'll give you half-a-crown. I'm sorry your father didn't like the present I sent him!"

During this pantomime at Leeds I received a sad blow in the death of my mother. My father had died in 1910, and mother had survived him but a few years.

It had been my mother's rule always to come and see me in a new part, and this year 1915 she travelled to Leeds alone in spite of age - she was then eighty. I remember how I met her at the station, and she was very late in arriving, and I was rather anxious as it was almost time for the show. Consequently, I had to drive her direct to the theatre and it was then that she gave me the last proof of what a marvellous memory she had.

As we approached the theatre she said, "Why, this is 'King Charles's Croft'" - and I, though I had been playing for several days at the theatre, did not even know the name of the street!

A day or two later she insisted on going over to Knaresboro' to see "Mother Shipton's Cave." I drove her there in my car, but in spite of all my precautions she caught a chill, and within a week she died. I brought back her body to London and laid her to rest in the same grave as my father in Norwood Cemetery.

The regard in which she was held was universal, and I and other members of my family were the recipients of countless condolences.

There is one, which I reproduce here, which I treasure especially. It was written by Mr H. Ormonde, who was personal bodyguard for many years to Queen Alexandra. So touching a tribute to the memory of a great and noble woman it is indeed, and one so eloquently descriptive of her character, that I make no apology for quoting it in full.

Dated from Leeds, on January 9th, 1915,- Mr Ormonde then had retired and was living in Leeds – and addressed to me at the Theatre Royal, Leeds, where I was playing in the pantomime "Cinderella", the letter reads:

"*My dear Mr. Kitchen,*

Permit me to offer you my sincere and respectful sympathy in the loss of your mother, who was a venerated friend of mine, for considerably over forty years. Indeed a landmark has been removed. She showed me a personal kindness, when I was quite a youth that I can never forget, and I am positive that anyone, like I then was, alone and a stranger in London, could always feel that if they knew her they had a reliable, kind and cheerful friend in her.

I remember in the early eighties when I was at Lord Granville's at Carlton House Terrace, I used to talk to her every day, and she would show me the letters from your brother, who was fulfilling an engagement in Russia, a wonderful thing in those days.

When I moved up to Marlborough House, she was always glad to see me, and talk of events and people. I remember seeing the three young princesses (now Queen Maude, the Princess Royal and Princess Victoria) stopping and talking to her more than once and their playful young brother George, now our Gracious King, would play some pranks, and make her laugh, and I remember how politely he lifted his hat and bowed to her, after he had been away a long time and grown she did not recognise him, and when I said it was Prince George, she told me how affable he was, and what merry blue eyes he had.

When I got to Buckingham Palace I did not see so much of her, but often had a chat. I think all the Royalties and aristocracy in London knew her, and I remember Queen Alexandra and the Duchess of Edinborough taking the present Emperor of Russia to see her.

She was always interested in the doings of society, and she hated and was greatly shocked by any scandal. She could not bear to condemn anyone, her heart was too good for that. About a certain great lady who made some sensation she said, "Ah, poor thing. I remember her as a child, like a fairy, so sweet and loveable; the temptations were too much."

Of another she said "a thousand left like her, without a mother, under bad influence, surrounded by flatterers, might have been worse. God help her, poor thing!" And so she spoke of all. Of course the really bad got no quarter from her.

I remember also the gracious and kindly interest our late King Edward took in her, and I once saw him leave his carriage at the Duke of York's steps and walk over and chat and laugh with her. While she had all the self-possession of a duchess, and such old-world courtesy – but such is life – links keep breaking.

Fred with his mother in 1914

I hope to see you personally some evening. God bless you and yours.

Yours very sincerely,
Henry H Ormonde

Royalty indeed have always been charming to my family and to me.

Following the pantomime came a new sketch, - "All Eyes," - then "Billy Crusoe" in "Robinson Crusoe" with the Moss Empires, and after that a part in Sir Oswald (then "Mr") Stoll's spectacular revue "Look Who's Here!" at the London Opera House. In the large and brilliant cast of this revue were two clever dancers called Caryll and Hyde. It was due to an accident that happened to me in this show that Billy Caryll became a star.

I had to do a bit of knockabout business with Billy Merson, in which I dived over the footlights into a private box. One night I was doing this and failed to see a chair in the shadow of the box, and caught the bridge of my nose on it, putting myself hors de comedian. That night I was made up with the last of some German grease paint I had acquired somewhere in my travels, and it got into the wound. I managed to play for two or three nights, but the swelling and the pain got steadily worse.

As I sat in my dressing room before the show on the third or fourth night I felt really ill. I had a terrible pain around the nose and eyes and my head ached to a degree that was almost intolerable. But at the same time I should probably have gone on, because I expected the pain would pass - it seemed such a slight accident - but Harry Vernon (the author of "Mr. Wu") happened to come in. "Good heavens, Fred," he exclaimed. "You look as though you're going to die. You can't go on like that. How d'you feel?"

I explained and he said. "Wait a minute. I'll get somebody to look at you. Don't dress yet. Wait quietly till I get back."

I was ready enough to do that, and he went away, to return a few minutes later with a stranger, who proved to be an eminent Harley street specialist. He examined my face and looked grave.

"The grease-paint has got into the wound," he said, "and what you have there is about as dangerous a case of blood-poisoning as I've seen. It's spreading quickly and will soon reach the brain. Unless you have it operated on within twenty-four hours you'll be dead! Have you got a good doctor?"

Startled and scared, I said I had.

"Then go home at once and send for him," he said. "And let him get that poison out of your system right away. It's a simple operation and if it's done at once you'll be all right."

That was enough for me. Off I went, and called at my doctor's house on the way. Luckily he was in; he operated on me at once; and I went home to bed.

One does not get over a thing like that in a minute or two, and it was hardly surprising that I could not go to the show on the following day, nor for several days. But a couple of days or so after the operation, Mr. Stoll sent along one of his managers, Mr. Llewellyn Johns, to ask me to get back as soon as I possibly could, as my understudy was not doing very satisfactorily and there was a real need for me in the show.

I explained that I would like to get back at once, but was honestly not fit enough to go on again and probably wouldn't be for a few days. "But," I said, "you've got a man there who could play my part excellently. He's been in my dressing room sometimes and mimicked me in the part for fun, and given as good an impersonation of me as ever I've seen. And he says he knows the part from A to Z. Why not put him on?"

"Yes, I know whom you mean" Johns said, "but he's a dancer, not a comedian."

"Yes, I know," I replied, "but he can do it and he does know the part. Give him a trial."

The upshot of it was that they did give him a trial. He went on and played the part of everybody's satisfaction until I was well enough to go back.

Then came the end of the run of "Look Who's Here" at the London Opera House and I was due to return to Moss Empires. "Look Who's Here" went to the Coliseum for two weeks and was then scheduled to go on tour for a few more weeks, and the young dancer who had played the part so well dissolved partnership with the other member of their double act and went with the show in my part and played it as he had played it in my absence.

That was the start of Billy Caryll as a comedian. Today he is a top-liner with a partner, Miss Hilda Munday, playing together as Caryll and Munday.

A fine old friend of mine who came into the show a few weeks before it ended was Arthur Roberts, and I was delighted to see him arrive, and he was no doubt equally pleased to see me, for we had been friends for so many years. A special part had been introduced into the show for him and he and I had to work together. We had a duet in the first act and another in a later scene. In the latter Arthur was playing a little "midinette" and I played a sort of roué of the Boulevards.

This second duet was in French.

Naturally, with all my past experience on the Continent, I had no hesitation in tackling a little thing like this, and as I had always been under the impression that Arthur was an even better French scholar than myself, I said to him when we talked it over first. "Well, that won't be any trouble to us, Arthur, singing a duet in French, will it? When shall we rehearse it?"

Arthur suggested Monday.

We met on Monday.

Said Arthur, "Well, Fred, perhaps we'd better slip over and have one little toothful before we start."

"That's a good idea," I agreed.

So we adjourned to the hotel at the back of the theatre.

After we had our "toothful" and then another toothful, and then two more, Arthur suggested that it was getting a bit late, and we might as well put off the rehearsal till the following morning.

What, after all, was a French duet and a bit of French patter to experienced Continental actors like us? And, anyway, we had a week before us for rehearsal. So I agreed readily.

On the morrow we met again - same time, same place.

Said Arthur, "Well, Fred, perhaps we'd better slip over and have one little toothful before we start...."

"That's a good idea."

So we adjourned to the hotel at the back of the theatre.

And ... after having two little toothfuls and then two more, Arthur suggested that we should put off the rehearsal until the following day.

What, after all, was a little French duet and a bit of French patter to a couple of linguists like Arthur and me? And we had several days left for rehearsal. So I agreed.

Next day we met again - same place, same time.

Said Arthur, "Well, Fred...."

And so every morning that week we repeated the ceremony, and still we hadn't begun our rehearsal. But what, after all, is a mere French duet and bit of French patter to a couple of real old-timers who spoke the language like Arthur and me....

Saturday came. By this time, I really did think we ought to do something about it. Rehearsals are part of our job, after all....

So on Saturday I said to him, "Look here, Arthur; we've got to get on with this duet. We've got to sing it on Monday."

"Oh," said Arthur gaily, "that'll be all right, Fred. What are you going to have?"

We parted on the understanding that I would call for him at his home at Camden Town on Sunday morning, take him back with me to lunch at my own home in Dulwich, collect the music, and we could get on with the rehearsal.

That Saturday night I shall always remember. It was the night of the great Zepp air raid on London when they dropped bombs all over the place. One fell on a tram at Streatham and seventeen people were killed.

That night my wife, my brother and two of my children were with me in the car when I went home. I stopped at Brixton to put down my brother, who lived near the town hall there. He crossed the road; I watched him for a moment and then started off again, and ... CRASH! I had not gone two hundred yards when a bomb fell on the very spot where a moment or two before the car had stood.

That it missed us I still regard as a miracle ... another moment's delay ... a second's hesitation about the opening of the door ... another word or two of goodnight ... and that bomb would have dropped precisely on top of the car ... and ... good-night, the Kitchen family....

Two minutes later another bomb fell on a house on Brixton Hill that had once been the home of peel, the billiards player.

And then, horror added to horror, a thousand yards or so in front of us, another bomb fell on a tramcar. It was the bomb which killed seventeen people and injured a good many more. We did what we could, and finally I got my wife and children home ... but I hope I never live through another Saturday night like that.

Anyway, I called at Camden Town on Sunday morning. Arthur Roberts threw his arms around me and said, with a little catch in his throat that I shall ever remember, "My dear boy, I never expected to see you. I heard of the terrible accident out your way last night. I thought you were dead. I was so positive you were dead I have eaten no breakfast - only a whisky and soda!"

Arthur wanted to drive around and look at the damage the German bombs had done. We had a run round and he listened while I told him the story of the horrors of the night.

Then he thought he would like to go to Norwood Cemetery and look at my father's grave ....

(He often said that it was my father who had taught him all that he knew of mime.)

We went to the cemetery.

The gates were closed.

But although the gates were shut, the "Thurlow Arms" - a very friendly place "within the meaning of the Act" and happily situated very near to the cemetery - was open.

Arthur suggested that as, after all, we were on our way to lunch - and to learn the duet! - a little toothful would perhaps be appropriate.

So into the Thurlow Arms we went.

As we entered, the jovial landlord, one Edward Auckland, descried us, came up to me cheerily and said, "Fred, isn't that Arthur Roberts?"

I admitted that it was, whereupon Auckland said, "When I was a lad, Arthur Roberts was a sort of a God to me. Please introduce me."

So I introduced Auckland to Roberts, and we moved over to the bar to order drinks; but before we could do so, the landlord exclaimed, "Half a minute. I know what Mr. Roberts likes." Without another word, he disappeared into the cellars and a minute later came back with three quarts of the most delicious champagne I have ever tasted.

From this point the story becomes a bit difficult to tell, because the memory on which I pride myself fails me here a little ....

I know we were two hours late for lunch, but I have a very charming and patient wife and we were forgiven. (And anyway, it wasn't the only time it ever happened!)

After lunch we adjourned to the drawing-room to learn the duet.

Arthur produced a foolscap sheet with some red dots on one side and some black dots on the other. Sticking it on the piano he said, "Now, Fred, the red ones are yours and the black ones are mine."

Perhaps that excellent champagne had something to do with it, but it was too much for me.

"What is it?" I asked.

"The duet," he said, and began to tap it out with one finger on the piano ....

"La di da da – that's you."

"La di de de dee – that's me."

"La de doo dee – that's you. You see how it goes."

Yes, I saw. He had written it all out in two-colour tonic sol-fa, and that, apparently, was all he knew about it. Which only goes to show what a great artiste he was.

But there was worse to come.

"Yes, but what about the words? Where are the words, Arthur?"

"We make our own words."

And that was the first time I knew that Arthur Roberts' wonderful French was only spoof French.

But was it good?

I claim to speak French. I can speak it as well – and some say much better – than I speak English, but it sounded like French to me. I wish I could reproduce it – but nobody but Arthur Roberts could possibly do that.

Just to show how marvellously he got away with it, here I must interpolate the story of when he went to a big affair at which the late King Edward, then Prince of Wales, was present. Arthur was introduced to a French noble and at once made a wonderful speech in French - his own spoof French, of course.

This French nobleman afterwards remarked to the Prince. "What beautiful French Mr. Roberts speaks - but I cannot understand from what province of France he comes!"

To return to the duet. The Monday night arrived. Luckily we had to sing the number before a front cloth, so I got the stage manager to cut a small opening about the size of the mouth of a pillar-box in the cloth and put a garden seat in front of it, so that when Arthur and I met on the stage we could sit on the garden seat and the stage manager could stand behind and prompt us through the hole.

After we had finished the song we were complimented by our musical director, who said we had never missed a word of either patter or song!

Chapter XXI

The period immediately following my engagement at the London Opera House I do not look upon as of any particular importance. The war was still playing havoc with the profession and I suppose that the theatres were really suffering from the restlessness that permeated the world during those momentous years. Certainly it seemed difficult to settle down. I, for one, although I was still safely sheltered from the worst difficulties by my contract with Moss Empires, found it something of a problem to decide what to do, what to put on, just how would be the best way to carry on. I had all the old proved successes available, I had practically carte blanche to do what I liked within my own province; and yet, times seemed to have changed so much that I found myself wondering whether they would be received as well as ever. Undoubtedly, I felt the very character of the music hall was changing.

In fact, the decline of the music hall, so apparent in the years that succeeded the war, had already begun. It was due, not so much, I think, to the reasons most generally given, - the ever-growing cinema, the ever larger buildings, the lack of outstanding stars, - but much more to the fact that during the war newcomers, who lacked the necessary long experience necessary for great success, crept into the variety profession, as they crept into a score of other trades and callings. This, perhaps, was the immediate outcome of those false boom years when money flowed like water, and profits were to be had for the taking. But their ultimate result was failure.

Now at last, I think, after the lean times, the wheel is turning full circle, and the music hall is coming back into popular favour. Variety has installed itself on the cinema stage; people are coming once more to realise the study, the thought, the art that goes to the making of vaudeville entertainment. After being long ignored, or at least overshadowed, by the more modern and cheaper cinema and radio, it is coming into its own again. The signs are there, and I hope I am reading them aright, for I would gladly see the music halls surge up on the high tide of prosperity again. Ours is an ancient and an honourable art. Once, professional jesters were the sole prerogative of kings; to-day the modern jester, comedian of the music halls, is permitted to amuse the world, and only desires that the world, - and his wife, - shall come and be amused.

This disquisition by the way; what I set out to express was a sort of dissatisfaction I felt with the material I had at my disposal in these newer, changing times.

I acquired new sketches, and toured in them very successfully and profitably, but felt the whole time very restless. The opening of the year 1918, however, brought a change for me. Albert de Courville, at that time, was producing a big revue for Moss Empires at the Folies Bergères in Paris.

He asked me to come along and see him and talk it over, and after a few minutes chat it was arranged that I should join him as principal comedian, with Shirley Kellogg as principal lady and a cast which included also

Winnie Melville, Irene Browne, George Clarke, Florence Smithers, and that great little Australian comedienne, Daphne Pollard. There were also several other English performers for minor parts and also an English troupe of dancers and the "Manchester Mites." The rest of the cast was to be composed of French artistes engaged in Paris by Mr. de Courville.

This sounded better. I was delighted, for many reasons. Principally, perhaps, because I was offered a princely salary - always a great remover of depression - but also because I still had a fondness for Paris that had grown out of all the good times and experiences - as well as the occasional bad times - I had spent there during my life. I had, too, tremendous confidence in de Courville, so that my pleasurable anticipations could not be marred by even the slightest doubts. I knew that his production would be fine, and would be successful, and I was equally confident of my own reception in the French capital. There was also that happy expectation of renewing many old associations. Finally, there was the prospect of entertaining thousands of our own lads spending their leave in Paris.

So my spirits rose again and I set off with my wife for Paris, filled once again with the happiest anticipations to fulfil the six-months' contract I had signed with Mr. de Courville. It was the first time I had played at the Folies Bergères and that fact alone would be calculated to give any old pro a thrill.

The opening night of "Zig-Zag" was a thrill. The "Folies" was packed. Three-quarters of the audience was in khaki. They were the boys from home; the boys from Canada; the boys from Australia and New Zealand.

My opening scene was in French. It was the second scene of the revue. I had to play the scene with a French artiste; and since I am not a Frenchman I hardly expected more of a reception than "the claque." I must explain this "claque." There is a "chef de claque," a man who is paid by the management and allowed each night a given number of free tickets. His duty is to bring in a number of people and place them in seats selected carefully on either side of the theatre. Then, when the "chef" thinks the moment appropriate, he gives a signal and the "claque" start the applause. It is an old French custom. The claque has been employed in France as long as my experience in France carries me. It has also been tried out in London at the Empire and Alhambra theatres in Leicester Square: that was in the days when they used to run big ballets there.

So, when on that memorable night, I made my entrance on that famous stage for the first time in my life, you can imagine perhaps the sudden intensity of my feelings as the house burst out in a roar of "Good old Fred!" "Good old Fred!" "Good old Fred!" in a dozen loud, uproarious, frenzied dialects. I heard it in Lancashire, in Yorkshire, in Cockney, and Scotch and even in Irish. It came in a tremendous burst of enthusiasm from every part of the house so that I almost staggered under it. What a welcome! A lump came into my throat with the pleasure of it. For a whole minute - a years-long minute - I stood there unable to go on, while the enthusiasm rolled about me and overwhelmed me. Never, when at long last it had quieted down a bit, did I feel less like being funny. I felt more like crying - like weeping for the lads out there - the lads from the trenches - who so wholeheartedly, generously and vociferously welcomed my presence among them.

The show was a tremendous success, and before it was half over both Mr. Frank Allen, the managing director of Moss Empires, Ltd., and Mr. R.H.Gillespie, who had both come to Paris for the opening night, came round to my dressing room to compliment me on my terrific reception. In fact, so great was the success of "Zig-zag" that night that an enterprising gentleman the following day bought up all the bookable seats for three or four months – and what greater success can any man want? He sold them nightly outside the Folies Bergères. This meant, that if you required a seat, you had to go to him and pay what he liked to ask. Seats that would have cost the equivalent of ten shillings were selling then for about thirty five - and he sold them like hot cakes!

The company soon settled happily down to the prospects of a long run. Everybody was cheerful and the spirit of war-time Paris - war-time gay Paris - was over all of us. The tens of thousands of our boys, who in those hectic days would come to the French capital to spend their short leaves, gave often an almost English colouring - not to say character - to the place. It was one of my delights in the morning to sit outside a café on one of the Boulevards and talk with them. It was a wonderful experience to gather a dozen or more of them around me and listen to their stories of the war, of their ordeals, of their experiences. I made it a habit to entertain as many as possible every day to lunch, and always there would be half a dozen or more whom I knew or who at any rate knew me.

Echoes of those days still come back to me. Not long ago, I was walking through Leicester Square, a man in a large car stopped, called me, and said, "Mr. Kitchen, you wouldn't remember me. I was a sergeant in the Army during the war, and one day you pulled me up on the Boulevard and stood me some drinks and a lunch. I shall never forget it, because I was absolutely broke at the time. Now, I should like you to come along and have something with me."

Many of the boys have I met since, and always they have told me of the pleasure I was able to give them in those strange days, and have been anxious to show their appreciation of what little I was able to do to brighten their lives, at least for a passing moment.

Armistice came while "Zig-Zag" was still at the height of its success, and with me, as I suppose with millions of others, the day stands out in my memory as the most astounding, the most ecstatic, the most frenzied day in history. Though in a hundred cities the wildest scenes took place, I doubt if anywhere else in the world they excelled in their amazing vividness the wild exhilaration of the Paris crowds. All traffic was prohibited and the streets surged with masses of excited soldiers and civilians. Flags of the nations appeared by thousands, as if by magic. French and English, Belgian and Portuguese, Italian and Scotch - officers and men of all the Allied nations poured in jabbering groups and wild crowds up and down the boulevards. What mattered it that they did not understand each other's languages? Nothing. They were the gayest, lightest-hearted crowds the world has ever seen, shouting, laughing, gesticulating, dancing, happy.

And at the theatre at night! As I entered the vestibule to start with, I saw a group of Canadian soldiers dancing on the grand piano, and crash! they all went through. End of piano. During the show, men and officer, crazily excited, kept jumping over the footlights and on to the stage to join in the show. And they joined in. It was the craziest show ever, and would have left Mr. George Black's "crazy weeks" at the Palladium looking as tame as a funeral service by comparison. How the show finished I never knew. I gave it up as a bad job long before the end and left the audience to finish it off! Besides, I was feeling as excited as everyone else! M. Arnould, one of the high officials of the Folies Bergères, a Belgian who had earlier in the war done his bit, had been captured by the Germans and escaped, during the show had joined me in my dressing room. He had draped himself in a huge Belgian flag, and I, to keep him company, made a similar use of a Union Jack. We got hold of a Scotsman who played the bagpipes in the revue, and promised him a hundred francs an hour to come with us.

Out into the streets we went with our piper, leaving the show to look after itself. The piper tuned up, and with Arnould and myself on either side of him, we marched triumphantly along, the old pipes skirling wonderfully. Then we ran into a group of English officers, they surged about the piper, snatched him from us bodily, surged away into the crowd - and that was the last we saw of our piper for twenty-four hours!

A night or two afterwards I arrived back at the hotel from the show with my wife, and there, standing on the hotel steps, was Fred Kitchen, Junr., now aged sixteen.

Considering that we had fondly believed him to be at school at Dulwich College, we were justifiably surprised. In a properly stern and parental manner I demanded an explanation.

"Oh, it's all right, Dad," he said cheerfully, "I thought I'd like to come and see you and Mum, so I borrowed £8 from the headmaster, and here I am!"

Many strange things occurred in connection with war souvenirs in those days of enthusiasm, as we all remember, but none came within my own experience stranger than this, which occurred in a café opposite the Folies Bergères.

I was sitting there one morning with a fellow called Charlie Stern, when a couple of English Tommies came along. They seemed a bit the worse for wine and we watched them as they ordered their drinks.

When the drinks came, one of them seemed to have some difficulty finding the money to pay for it, and began turning his pockets out on to the little marble table at which they were sitting. First he put down some letters and papers, and then a huge handful of Iron Crosses!

But he found his money, they drank their drinks, leisurely and finally rose to go. As the man who had paid picked up the Iron crosses, an American officer who had also been watching them, walked over to him and said, "Say, sonny, you've got a lot of Iron Crosses there. Can I have a look at one?"

With some reluctance, the man handed him one, and the officer, after looking at it rather enviously, suggested that he would like one.

"Say, you've got a lot of them there, sonny. Couldn't you spare one. I'd like to take it back with me."

"No," said the tommy, "they're for the old folks. There's one for my father, one for mother - and so on." He went through a list of relations long enough for two families.

But the officer was persistent and finally the other Tommy joined in. "Go on, Bill. It's no good giving them to the kids. They'll have forgotten all about 'em by the time they grow up."

"Oh, well," said Bill, as he turned to the officer again. "perhaps I might spare one, but I couldn't let you have it under a hundred francs."

"That's O.K."

And a hundred franc note changed hands.

While this conversation had been going on, the proprietor of the café had joined them and was examining one of the crosses. He invited the two Tommies to have another drink, which they did, and then he said he would like one of the souvenirs, too, but he thought a hundred francs was more than he could afford. But, if the English soldat would take seventy....

Bill demurred. "Go on," said the other Tommy, "you can spare another all right."

"Oh, all right, then," said Bill, "only little Bert won't 'ave it, that's all."

A few minutes afterwards Stern and I left the café and I noticed that the two lads with the Iron Crosses were standing on the pavement quite near. I said to Stern "I'd like one of those Crosses myself. It'll be a nice souvenir to have in years to come. Go and see if they'll sell me one. I wouldn't mind paying seventy to a hundred francs."

So Charlie went up to them where they stood looking at the big electric signs on the front of the Folies Bergères opposite - the names of Shirley Kellogg and Fred Kitchen - and said, "D'you know Fred Kitchen?"

"'Course we know Fred Kitchen," said the lad with the Iron Crosses. "Why?"

"Well, will you let him have one of those Crosses. He'd like to buy one from you."

"Why, where is he?"

Charlie Stern pointed me out and the tommies came over.

"Are you Fred Kitchen?"

I admitted it, as we shook hands.

"Glad to know you," said Bill. "I've heard you many a time in Birmingham. Hope I'll hear you there again many a time as well."

I told him I'd like to buy one of his souvenirs.

"You don't want one of those things," he said, with a wink. "Wait till you get back to Birmingham. You can get a dozen for eight bob"

That night when I went to the theatre Daphne Pollard said: "Fred, guess what I've got for a souvenir to-day."

"What?" I asked, "an iron cross?" She looked surprised. "Yes, how on earth did you guess?"

"What did you pay for it?" -

"A hundred francs. Cheap, wasn't it, for a thing like that?"

I told her where it had come from, but she didn't believe me, and I expect she still treasures it among her mementoes of the Folies Bergères.

Chapter XXII

After "Zigzag" I played in three more of de Courville's revues: "Hotch-Potch" at the Duke of York's, "Same to You" on tour, and "Jig-Saw" at the London Hippodrome.

It was in this show that Maisie Gay and I introduced a little sketch which afterwards became a sort of stock-in-trade and which I played hundreds of times. This was "Washing the Baby," and the way it developed from a tiny lightning revue act into a permanent and popular sketch was, to say the least of it, unusual.

Wal Pink, part author with Edgar Wallace of the revue, said he wanted a new little act. I suggested that I had occasionally done a farcical bit of business of washing a baby in pantomime, which might make a neat quick little act, if he would write some snappy lines for it. He did and provided about four minutes of dialogue. This we played the first night, and it went over so well that we could not resist the temptation to add a few spontaneous gags that were not in the script. The second night it ran for six minutes; next night for nearly ten, and by the end of the week we were "washing the baby" for a good twenty-five minutes, while the house rocked with laughter. So well did it go that it was soon established as the principal sketch of the revue, and when "Jig-Saw" was over Maisie

Fred in Jig-Saw

Bathing the Baby

Gay and I toured Moss Empires with it as a top-of-the-bill turn.

I cannot pass over my association with Maisie Gay in this sketch without paying a sincere tribute to her wonderful qualities as an actress. Her versatility was amazing. She was one of the best pathetic actresses I have known, and in low comedy parts I do not think she has ever had a superior. She could play any part, and play it wonderfully well. I believe if she had been asked to go through a star-trap, or do a flying-trapeze turn, she would have made a very good attempt at either!

What is more, she was as clever and brilliant off the stage as she was on it, which is by no means always the case. Her sense of humour and her sparkling wit enlivened every party, and probably no one was more sought after in the profession than this young actress whose name fitted her so perfectly.

Our partnership in "Washing the Baby" had to come to an end in 1921, as Maisie had another contract to fulfil. In January 1922 I re-joined forces with my old friend and producer, Fred Karno, in a revue he was producing entitled "1922."

Twelve years had passed since our old association had been severed, but we had always maintained a friendly acquaintance, and I think I am right in saying, a high regard for each other's abilities.

This revue, "1922," was very successful; Marie Blanche was the leading lady, and the now famous broadcasting star, Elsie Carlisle, was in the cast.

The second week we were at the New Cross Empire, and it was here that I was as neatly hoaxed by a practical joker as I have ever heard of anyone being. Earlier in this

story I have told how Karno, with his natural genius for showmanship, contrived novel publicity stunts. In this case the stunt was merely a lucky fluke for the practical joker, but Karno contrived to-turn it into a smart publicity trick.

I was sitting in my dressing-room at the Empire after first house on the Monday evening. In the room with me were Marie Blanche and Fred Karno, the manager of the theatre, and one or two visitors who had dropped in to congratulate us on the show. The hall-keeper came in and said that a gentleman was asking to see me.

On nights like that everybody was welcome, and without asking his name I said, "Bring him in."

The stranger arrived. No sooner had he entered than he threw out his hands and cried, "Fred, my old pal. It's good to see you again. I haven't seen you for fifteen years!"

He certainly hadn't! I couldn't place him at all, but I had to be polite.

"Well, well," I welcomed him. "I'm glad to see you. Have a drink. Have you met Miss Blanche... and Mr. Karno... and...." In short, I introduced him all round.

Then, wondering if perhaps his answer would give me a clue as to whom he was, I asked, "What have you been doing yourself?"

"Oh," he said cheerfully, "I've been all over the world since I saw you last, and I've brought back a wonderful act."

A few more minutes of general conversation and then he said, "I tell you what. I'd like to show you one of my little tricks, if you've got a minute. It's a marvel. It'll get 'em cold."

"What is it?"

"Oh, it's quite simple. Only takes. a minute." Then, turning to Marie Blanche, he said, "you wouldn't mind being handcuffed to Mr. Kitchen for a moment, would you?"

She looked a trifle dubious, but he insisted it was only for a moment and it wouldn't hurt.

So we were handcuffed together!

Then said my returned stranger, "Now, this is what I want you to do. You count ten. I go out of the room while you are counting. When you've finished counting ten - mind you, you've got to say it exactly together! - you say sharply, "They're off" - and the cuffs will fall to the ground.

It sounded easy. We obeyed instructions ... started counting ten ... he left the room ... we cried, "They're off!" ... and ... nothing happened.....

We counted again ... cried "They're off!" again they weren't....

"Well, there's a. rotten trick," said somebody.

I began to wonder. "Call that chap in," I said.

But he was not there. I sent for the hall-keeper.

"Have you seen that fellow who was here a few minutes ago? Go and find him – quickly..."

"He's gone," he said "Went out of the theatre two or three minutes ago."

We struggled to get those "bracelets" off. By this time we were all in a bit of a panic, for whatever happened we still had to play in the second house, and it was obvious that we had been beautifully caught. I asked somebody to go and find a policeman - he might have a key that would open hand-cuffs - but somehow there wasn't even a policeman to be found.

"Well," I said, "where's the nearest police-station?"

It proved to be at Blackheath. "Then we've got to go to Blackheath, quickly. Get a taxi, somebody."

Very much embarrassed, and accompanied by Rhodes Parry, the manager of the theatre, who did his best to keep an inquisitive stage-door crowd at bay, we clambered with difficulty into the taxi and off to the station we went. I explained to the Inspector in charge what had happened. Luckily he believed me.

"We'll soon have them off for you," he said when he had stopped laughing.

But it was not so easy. They must have been foreign handcuffs, for although the inspector's key released the one on Miss Blanche's wrist, that on mine definitely refused to respond to treatment and it began to look very much as though I should either have to wear it through the second house or miss the show and wait until the thing could be filed off.

It was a good fifteen minutes and a good many keys and implements had been tried before finally they succeeded in removing the contraption and we were able to go back to the theatre. By this time the story of the hoax had leaked out, - it was much too good to keep quiet about, and anyway Fred Karno wasn't missing a chance like that. We had a great reception.

Now it happened that the stranger had left behind him a little pocket-book containing a few private notes and £2 in money. Karno sent this to the police-station and every day for a week advertised in the "agony" columns that unless the money was claimed it would be given to the police orphanage.

It was never claimed!

When the tour with Fred Karno came to an end I took out an old sketch, "If the Cap Fits," with Marie Blanche as my leading lady. I managed to take a brief holiday in August, which I spent very amusingly in the company of my old pal Ben Albert, - the same who played with me as one of the Ugly Sisters at the Grand, Fulham, years and years before.

I picked Ben up early one evening, and we spent several entertaining, if not exactly profitable, hours together. One of these, incidentally, we passed in the company of Harry Tate and Wal Pink, causing them to be seriously late for a rehearsal at the Empire! Then Ben decided he would like to have a supper of jellied eels.

"I'll take you to a wonderful place," he promised. "You tell your chauffeur to drive to the Elephant and Castle, and then I'll direct him."

In due time we found ourselves at the Elephant, and under Ben's direction went a little further till he stopped us outside a shop. Out of the car we got, and went in.

A very handsome, dignified woman was talking to two younger women.

Said Ben importantly: "Come on, Ma. Two large basins of jellied."

The woman stared at us in surprise, but said nothing. I thought she was hardly the type one would expect to see in a jellied eel shop.

"Come on, Ma," Ben repeated impatiently. "Don't mess about. Two big basins of jellied."

The two younger women in the shop looked rather stunned, but the older one advanced with perfect calm. Addressing Ben she said. quietly: "Sir, I think you have made a mistake. This is a milliner's shop!"

We left, - two very crestfallen comedians, Ben muttering, "Well, Fred, it was a jellied eel shop once, and a dam' good one!"

We were neither of us feeling too good the next morning but after lunch at the Playgoers' Club things appeared brighter.

Ben said: "Now where shall we go?"

I suggested Paris. I had still two clear days' holiday in front of me. Ben didn't take it seriously, but he was willing enough to go wherever I said. I telephoned to Croydon and booked two seats on the next 'plane, and took Ben along to the aerodrome. We were introduced to Major Foote, that brilliant pilot who was later killed in the air race round England. He was to pilot the Paris 'plane that day. We climbed in, but still Ben could not really believe that we were going. He took it for one of my leg-pulls and was waiting to see where the joke was.

After a while he said: "Now, when are they going to turn us out?"

I said: "Look through the window!"

He looked. "Blimey!" he ejaculated. "We're up!" and we were.

When we got to Paris we were taken into the little office at Le Bourget and were asked to show our passports.

I never thought of passports!

This wasn't so easy to explain. People aren't supposed to get into aeroplanes and fly across the

Channel without thinking about passports. It was not long before a somewhat heated argument was going on, in French, and Ben, sitting in a chair and listening with a weirdly puzzled air, suddenly broke in with the question, "Wot's 'e talking about, Fred?"

I explained that we had no passports and it was on the cards we should be sent back without being allowed to go into Paris at all.

"Blimey," he said. "That don't matter - passports - does it?"

I told him that it certainly did.

"Here," he said, "show 'im this." He fumbled in his pockets and drew out an official looking document.

"What is it?" I asked.

But I could see. It was his dog licence!

"That'll show 'em who we are," he said. "It's got the lion and the unicorn on it - and that's good enough for anybody!"

All this while the other passengers were waiting in the aerodrome bus and were getting impatient, not to say furious, and eventually Major Foote came along to see what the delay was about. It was lucky for us that he did, for they took his word for our bona fides and he personally guaranteed that we would return to England on the ten o'clock liner the following morning, which we undertook to do.

In Paris, Major Foote took charge of us, and we were introduced to a good many of the flying boys, including Mr. McIntosh, who was to pilot us back the next day. And after spending a pleasant hour or two with them and enjoying an excellent dinner, I called a taxi and took Ben along to make the acquaintance of the Folies Bergères.

Ben got another shock.

No sooner had we entered the stage door than the concierge and her son rushed. to me and kissed me warmly on both cheeks. "Ah, c'est M. Kitchen!"

I enquired for my old friend M. Arnauld and was told he was in his office.

"Come along, Ben," I said, and along we went to the side of the stage, where I was immediately pounced upon by the master carpenter, who kissed me; some of the stage hands kissed me; the head fireman kissed me; one of the actors who had played with me in "Zig-Zag" in 1918 rushed up and embraced and kissed me, and it was quite a while before I could tear myself away from this exuberant welcome and make for M. Arnauld's office.

But I did at last, and as I knocked and entered, up jumped Arnauld and cried, "Ah, mon cher Fred!", threw his arms around me and kissed me loudly on both cheeks.

And I heard a disgruntled voice say behind me "Blimey, they're all cissies!"

Chapter XXIII

It was in October 1922 that the variety world lost the woman who can almost without fear of contradiction be described as its greatest star.

Never was there anyone like Marie Lloyd, and when at fifty-two she died, every one of us in the variety profession felt that we had lost someone who could never be replaced, as indeed we had, for she was a friend to all.

Joe Elvin summed it up as we talked while we followed in the funeral procession. "Poor old Marie," he said with genuine feeling, "we shall never have another like her."

Only a few weeks later Joe and I again suffered a personal loss in the death of Wal Pink. Joe and Wal had been intimate friends all their lives, and Wal had written more than a hundred sketches for Joe, and I do not think there was ever a flop among them.

Wal's death was unexpectedly sudden. Albert de Courville was producing a new revue at Sheffield and things had not been going too smoothly. He wired for Wal Pink to come up at once and give him a hand in person. Without even troubling to put on an overcoat when he received the summons, Wal jumped into his little car and set off there and then for Sheffield. It was an act of devotion to duty that cost him his life, for so cold was the day that Wal caught a chill from which he never recovered.

What a fine fellow he was. As genial, happy and friendly as he was clever. Liked and admired by everybody he, too, was a loss to his friends and to the profession in general which can never quite be replaced.

It was early in the following year, 1923, that, in cooperation with Mr. Norman Lee, I set out on an experimental tour with a three-act farce which was designed to play twice nightly. The show, called "Oh, Mabel!", occupied the whole of the bill to the exclusion of any of the usual turns, and though it was financially a success I never could quite rid myself of the feeling that a full-length play was somehow out of place in a twice-nightly music hall. But it ran, successfully enough, for a few months and, as I say, I made money out of it.

Then Edward Marriss and Harry Norris bought the rights of Wal Pink's "Hotch-Potch" from Albert de Courville. In this production of the old show I had Ouida Macdermott, the daughter of the famous "lion comique" Macdermott who sang that oft-quoted "We don't want to fight, but, by Jingo, if we do!" and Stephen Addison. This was the first time Stephen and I had appeared on the stage together since forty-two years before, which, on the face of it, seems strange - that two men could be in the same profession, and the same branch of that profession, all those years, working all that time in the same country, travelling round and about, crossing each other's paths in a dozen directions, and never meet.

"Hotch-Potch" again proved a sure winner and ran steadily along playing always to tip-top business, until February 1924. After that I put on "If the Cap Fits" again until the summer, and in July joined Herbert Darnley once more in a new show he had written called "Joan, All Alone." This show ran happily and profitably along for about ten months, when I was approached by a syndicate to play a comic opera called "Maid of the East" written by Davy Burnaby, Edward Lauri and Herbert C. Sargent with some additional lyrics by George Arthurs. The music was by the late William Neale who personally conducted.

Neale was a man for whose genius I had always the highest praise; he should have taken one of the highest places in the classical music world. But I fear that his opinion of my own musical ability would hardly have coincided with my opinion of his.

When we began rehearsals for this show, "Maid of the East," he tried hard to give me the "operatic" touch.

"But I don't know a note of music," I told him.

"That's all right," he said. "You can sing well enough if you try. Just try a scale."

I tried a scale, and he seemed to think I would do, though when I caught the sly smiles on the faces of one or two of the others in the cast I had my own doubts.

"Never mind," he said. "If you watch my baton and follow me carefully, it will be all right."

We managed through rehearsals somehow, though I fear he was far from happy about me, and there came "the night".

Now what with first-night nervousness and the unusual character of my part and the general excitement of the occasion, I was worried. I did my best. My first song was good stuff, and comic, and being myself a "comic" I was all right from that point of view – and I did try to follow Neale's baton, but by the end of the first half dozen bars something had begun to go wrong.

I tried to put it right; he tried to put it right, and it got worse. Another line or two and I was hopelessly out of time. I began to get a bit warm under the collar - so, I suppose, did he.

Another minute and it was worse still. I was lost. What to do? Nothing to do but gag it (and that isn't really done in comic opera!)

"Now, now," I said to the despairing conductor, as I stopped short in the song, "excuse me, there; wait a minute while I think of the words!"

I did it in my funniest voice and the audience howled.

But not so Mr. Neale.

With a look that blended contempt, despair, and injured dignity, he dropped his baton on to his music stand - and went!

I was left alone with the band. So I remarked to the audience, the stage, the orchestra and the world at large, "Now, that's better. He's gone, so we can get on with it."

It brought down the house and we did get on with it, but the offended conductor never spoke to me again, if he could help it. I don't think he liked comedians anymore!

After some three months "Maid of the East" came off and I went on tour with a musical play called "Week End," written by Walter W. Ellis. One of the places we visited was the Palace, Manchester, where I had so often appeared, and it was while I was here that I was tempted to take an active part in another profession - the profession of sport - and fell.

I happened one day to come across an old sporting friend of mine who owned greyhounds and he had the bright idea that if I acquired one or two and ran them successfully, not only should I make a good deal of money (!) but the glory and consequent publicity would do me a world of good. I had my doubts about the "successful" part of it, but he was a persuasive sort of a friend and - well, in the end, I fell.

"I've a nice little animal called 'Welcome June'," he said, "and you can have her for £40, and if she wins a few times in your name and you want to part with her, I'll take her back from you at the same price.

"Mind you," he added, "she's never won a race - but she's a likely winner."

It seemed fair enough, in spite of the last bit, and I closed the deal.

That week I ran "Welcome June" at Belle Vue in the Wordsworth Hurdles and in the betting she was in the "5 to 1 Others" class, but to everybody's surprise (and especially mine!) she won by four lengths. And during the week she ran altogether five times - and had two wins and two seconds!

It looked pretty good to me but a bargain was a bargain, and I had to let my friend have her back. "Welcome June" was sold to someone else in London and before she went to stud she had won no fewer than thirty-six races.

With a start like that I have, always felt a wee bit sorry I did not take up dog-racing seriously. I might have made a lot of money! (And of course I might not, but never mind that.)

As a matter of fact, I have always been keen on sport. Swimming; racing; boxing; I have done my share of all of them and enjoyed meeting the Champions. Many are the good friends I have made, for example in the boxing world. When I was quite young, I remember, I met Jem Mace. That was forty-four years ago and I was only nineteen. He owned a public house a few doors from the old Gaiety music hall in Birmingham, and with all the impertinence of youth I asked him questions that I would hardly dare to put to anyone in a like position now. He knew my father well, and also my uncle, Tom Lamb, who fought with the "raw 'uns." Many tales he told me of the old Prize Ring days and his mighty battles.

Before that, too, there was Jem Smith. Fifty years ago I saw him box with his brother at the Elephant and Castle theatre in the old sporting drama "Tom and Jerry." I met him again a little while before he died and we had a long talk about those days. He was much surprised to learn that I had seen him in the old play.

Charlie Mitchell was another champion of whom I saw a good deal in the old days at the Washington Music Hall, Battersea, when it was run by his father-in-law, "Pony" Moore (of Moore and Burgess Minstrels fame). Mitchell, by the way, was a brother-in-law of that popular comedian, Eugene Stratton, as they both married daughters of "Pony" Moore.

Remarkable man was Moore! He gave me once one of the most uncomfortable "breaks" I've had. It happened when I was playing in a dramatic sketch called "Donnybrook" at the Washington.

"Pony", it seemed, had a habit of telling his audience what a fine place it was and what wonderful people his performers were; and the week before we were due to play in this sketch, he had made a speech every night from the stage announcing the coming of the company and promising the audience the treat of their lives (as he did this every week, I've often wondered how much difference it made!) and announcing the play and the performers as the greatest ever.

It was Monday night. I was playing juvenile lead - Denis O'Dwyer, a young country farmer. In the middle of the play there is a dramatic scene. Everybody is on the stage. I, the hero, am denouncing the villain. It goes like this:

> O'Dwyer: Captain Vere, here before all these people, I wish to ask a straightforward question, and I demand a straightforward reply.
> Captain Vere (the villain): Indeed! And by what right?
> O'Dwyer: By the right that every honest man has to protect his wife's good name from the tongue of evil slander.

Follows inevitably a round of applause, especially strong from the gallery.

At this dramatic moment suddenly there is an interruption. Down the centre gangway of the hall comes Pony Moore. Right to the orchestra rail he advances. He holds up his hand, and his voice, with its strong American accent calls out:

"Just a minute, Kitchen. Stop a minute."

We all stop, startled and wondering if the theatre's on fire.

Tony turns his back on us and, facing the audience, he cries with upraised hand:

"Say, folks, what d'you think of 'em? Didn't I tell you last week how good they were? Can you beat 'em? No, of course you can't!

"Go on, Fred, get on with it!"

And with the last words he turns round to the stage, waving his hand, and then walks back the way he has come! But the "getting on with it" wasn't so easy after an interruption like that in the middle of one of the most dramatic incidents of the play!

Funny, of course; but I didn't think so just then. However, I did change my opinion when, after the show, he had all the company round to the bar and bought them all champagne! Pony Moore was like that.

It was twenty-five years ago that I met James Corbett (Gentleman Jim). I was playing the Empire, Newcastle, and he was at the rival music hall, the Pavilion, and on the Monday night he sent round a note to me saying, "Dear Kitchen - I have never met you, but I hear you're a good fellow. I'm here for a week, and I want a playmate. Can I call round and see you after the show?"

I sent over a warm invitation, as one professional to another, and he came around as soon as he was free. I took a liking to him on sight, and I think our feeling was mutual. They might well have called him "Gentleman Jim," for to look at him and talk to him no-one would have dreamed that he had ever been in the prize-ring. He had clean, well-cut features - none of the cauliflower ear business about Gentleman Jim - and a charming personality. Even his hands - those hands that had made mincemeat of many another face - were perfect. He was altogether one of the most likeable and entertaining men it has been my pleasure to meet.

We both happened to be going to Liverpool the following week, again in rival music halls, and although he had already made arrangements to stay at the Midland Hotel there, he cancelled those arrangements when he learned that I usually stayed at the Victoria, and booked rooms there so that we could continue our acquaintance.

I remember that it was while we were at Liverpool that he came to see me at a matinee accompanied by Little Tich, who luckily was also playing in Liverpool that week, and they made a remarkable double, as anyone can imagine, as they sat side by side in the stage box - the huge heavyweight pugilist and the diminutive comedian - but both great men. This was the week when we were expecting the fourth little Kitchen to arrive, and Jim said, "Now, listen, Fred. If it's a boy, you've got to call him James Corbett Kitchen."

Very early one morning he came to my bedroom before I was up, with a telegram in his hand, and said, "Fred, here's a wire. I expect the little thing's arrived."

I opened it - and we were both disappointed - for it was a girl!

He said, "Never mind, Fred. You can name her Jemima, and then for short you'll be able to call her Jim!"

So I sent the wife a wire: "Delighted you're both all right. Christening baby Jemima."

But before the day was out I got the reply I ought to have expected. It was short, but it was definite. It said, "You are not."

That settled that.

Other and later boxers whom I have met and liked have included Jimmy Driscoll; Freddy Welsh; that little wizard of boxing, Jimmy Wilde; and Jerry and Fred Delaney.

Speaking of Fred Delaney I recall that at Bradford once I was invited to a pantomime supper and ball. It was a real old-time party and it went merrily on till something like ten o'clock in the morning. But everything has to have an end and somewhere around that hour I might have been seen making my way back to my own hotel. As I walked that way whom should I meet but Fred Delaney who told me he was on his way to a photographer's to get some pictures done for use in connection with a trip he was going to make to try his luck in the United States.

I was still in party mood and suggested to him that, if he had any props with him in the little bag he was carrying, I would go along too and we'd have some photographs taken together. He said he had, and I went along. We had one or two pictures taken showing us sparring up to each other, and also one or two taken singly.

I thought no more of this until some few weeks later I was playing at the Coliseum in London. Getting to the stage door early one day for a matinee performance, I was astonished to find a remarkable group of people waiting for me. There wasn't a nose among them that might be taken for that of the Iron Duke, and most of them were decorated with the sign of the cauliflower ear.

Said one of them, as they gathered around me on sight, "What, there, old Fred!" and gave me such a playful punch on the ear as pulled me up short; and another handed me a couple of professional digs in the ribs that made me wonder what it was all about; and before I'd decided I had a nice light one under the chin - and all done so playfully and friendly-like that I could only stagger and say, "Here, what's all this about?"

"Well, me ole white 'ope," explained one. "You're the boy for us, you are."

It appeared they had seen in the current issue of "Boxing" one of those fatal photos of me sparring up to Fred Delaney and under it the caption, "Fred Kitchen – England's White Hope!" or something to that effect.

It cost me several drinks and the price of a whole packet of tickets for a benefit match at Hackney for one of their old bruiser pals to explain it away - and I think it was cheap at the price!

Fred told me afterwards that he had shown the photograph to the editor of "Boxing" and that gentleman had asked, surprised, "Who do you say this is?"

"That's Fred Kitchen - the new 'White Hope'."

"Good Lord!" said the editor, "it looks more like an antique dealer!"

But that didn't prevent him using it.

* * * * *

Early in 1926 I went out with a revue called, "Winning Ways" written by Firth Shephard, with Jean Allistone (the popular B.B.C. star and wife of the equally popular B.B.C. comedian, Tommy Handley) as leading lady.

It was, I suppose, a good enough show, but I would not put it among my big successes, although it went over fairly well and made money. Somehow I had come to feel the need of very special material for my work. Perhaps it was that with my long experience I had developed a style which authors found it difficult to fit. I always felt that I should be writing my own material, for who can understand a performer as he understands himself? And yet I couldn't.

With regard to that, I was feeling that I had written so much of my own comedy that I was written out, or else I was too conscious of an old philosophy of my father's, who used to say that "the brain is a book-case and when you have finished the last volume, you must go back to volume one - which is to repeat yourself!"

That may or may not be true, but the difficulty of finding the right stuff was apparent to others as well as to myself, and "Tristram" summed it up in the "Referee" of January 31, 1926, when he said:

> "There are few more resourceful and amusing comedians in the music-halls than Fred Kitchen. One cannot help regretting, therefore, that no author appears to be forthcoming who will provide him with a part in any way commensurate with his abundant ability.
>
> "Mr. Kitchen is the central figure in the touring show entitled "Winning Ways," which was at the Empire, Stratford, last week, but neither the author nor the producer of this "musical adventure" has shown much ingenuity in his own line of business.
>
> "Fortunately for the success of this musical comedy like piece, Fred has a big bag of tricks of his own into which he dips with no unsparing hand throughout "Winning Ways" and so afford

consolation for the absurdity of the "story" and the manner in which the show seems to drag when he is not on the stage."

This problem is one which besets the comedian always, and lucky is the man who can find for most of the time just the right material on which to base his own individual humour. For myself I have been fairly fortunate on the whole and I pay willing tribute to the authors who have provided me throughout my career with so much good and original material on which to build my work.

While I was playing in this particular show one of the most curious incidents of my career occurred. It all come out of a jocular remark made to a bright young journalist and though it brought me much publicity and caused a great deal of fun it also gave me a particularly worried half hour in deep water!

The young man had called to talk with me at the Hippodrome at Brighton where I was playing, and during the conversation something had been said about swimming the Channel. Just then a women who was a grandmother had either just done it or had made a pretty good attempt, and I said, "Well, I've just become a grandfather myself; I see no reason why I shouldn't try it. I can swim"

Just my little joke, but, as I have said, he was a bright young journalist, and perhaps I ought not to have been so surprised as I was when I read in a certain paper that "Fred Kitchen was training to swim the Channel. His attempt is to be made shortly."

Or when, that night, as I entered the theatre the hall-keeper told me I was wanted on the telephone from

London and when I answered the call I found that it was one of the picture papers asking whether during my stay at Brighton I was training for my forthcoming big swim. In a moment of recklessness I said yes, and the news editor at the other end asked me then what time I usually went out.

"As a rule," I said, "at six in the morning and again at one in the afternoon, "which was true enough in its way, for I generally made a point of getting some daily swimming in whenever I found myself playing at a seaside town.

So he said he would like to send a camera-man down the following day, and could I meet the man at the Hippodrome at twelve o'clock.

I said I would, wondering meanwhile where the joke was going to end, but expecting to get some fun out of it anyway, and early that next morning I set out to see what I could do about it. First I went and bought a real jazzy swimming costume - one that I thought would do justice to a prospective Channel-champion (though my courage failed me afterwards and I hadn't quite the nerve to wear it!) and then I went and had a little talk with the owner of the local bathing machines. And then I waited for my camera-man.

By the time he came the news had leaked out, and spread itself to some effect, too, for the beach was packed with people who apparently wanted to see the fun. Perhaps the fact that the bathing-machine man had found a nice long strip of red carpet to run from one of his machines to the edge of the sea had helped!

And all the time I knew well enough that the best I had ever been able to do was about three lengths up and down a swimming bath!

But it was too late to turn back and I duly came out on parade. Said the Press man, "What stroke do you intend to use, Mr. Kitchen?"

That was a bit of a poser, but "there was only one answer because I never could do more than three or four strokes overarm without shipping more water than was comfortable, so I said blithely, "The breast-stroke."

"The breast at stroke," he repeated, surprised. "I shouldn't have thought anyone could swim twenty-odd miles with the breast-stroke. You must be a wonder!"

"I am," I said.

"Well," he said, "don't go too far out. Just swim as far as that groin over there. I'll get some pictures of you in the water and then I'd like you to stand on the groin and I'll get a photograph of you about to dive."

It didn't look so difficult when I was standing on the beach. The groin he had pointed out seemed a mere twenty or thirty yards then. But in the water...... twenty miles seemed a better estimate.

Eventually, however, half dead, I did get there..... and that camera-man never knew what it cost me... somehow I managed to drag myself out of the water and clamber exhaustedly on to the groin..... I was beat....

But I was always a bit tough. In a minute or two I contrived to stand up and look as though I liked it..... and the photographer got his picture... but...

The worst, however, was yet to come. I couldn't very well walk back along the beach.

So into the water I had to go again....

How I did it I don't know to this day, for I was utterly exhausted. But somehow I struggled back and by dint of taking a good many rests floating on my back (and hoping they'd think on the beach that I was just disporting myself) I reached the red carpet once more..... but not before I'd made up my mind that that was the end of that joke!

I don't think the lookers-on thought much of my chances of success, either, and perhaps they weren't surprised when I announced, shortly afterwards, that my doctor had forbidden me, after all, to attempt the Channel!

Chapter XXIV

There is one form of acting which, in my opinion, has never received anything like its due share of praise, or, for that matter, of notice. All too often it is completely ignored by critic and commentator alike. I refer to the art of animal impersonation.

Earlier in this story I have had a good deal to say about one great animal impersonator - the versatile Charles Lauri, whose imitation of Sally, the Zoo chimpanzee, was so marvellous. Now, in pantomime at Wimbledon, where I played the title role in "Mother Goose" after "Winning Ways" finished at the end of the year, I had the delight of playing side by side with a man whose performance as the Goose was a piece of sheer genius.

That man was Fred Conquest, who, with his brother Arthur and their father, George Conquest, deserve to be classed among the most brilliant animal performers the world has ever seen.

Never shall I forget Fred Conquest's splendid acting in one scene particularly in "Mother Goose."

It was a scene in which I, the pathetic, ugly old Mother Goose, bewail my unhappy fate. Aged, decrepit, despised, alone, I sit miserably there on the stage. Nobody loves an ugly old woman like me.

The goose waddles over to my side and rubs his soft old head against me and flaps his wings and comforts me as he nuzzles his beak in my lap - and every action, every movement tells. It is difficult to describe, but I defy the hardest hearted to see that performance and not feel a lump come into his throat. Never once could I go through the scene without tears streaming down my face - and genuine tears, too, - and I have seen, through the little square of gauze which enabled Fred Conquest to see me out of his wonderful make-up, that he too was crying - and genuinely crying. And there were tears, too, in the audience - tears of sympathy and pity for poor old Mother Goose and tears of love for her wonderful, devoted old bird.

If that was not great acting, then I have never seen any. It was wordless acting, too; all pantomime with a mere piece of feathered "property". That prop was in itself a masterpiece. With what loving care it was handled! As Fred came off the stage, if only to go to his dressing room for a few minutes, his wife would throw a sheet over him with delicate care, lest the feathers on the goose should be accidentally ruffled, and always after the performance the prop would be most carefully hung up and covered.

It was the same with everything that any of the Conquests did. A good many people no doubt still remember George Conquest, the father, when he had the famous Grecian Theatre in the City Road, and even more will recall the days when he took over the equally famous Surrey Theatre, and the many dramas and pantomimes he produced there. Some of his marvelous make-ups in those pantomimes would astonish a present-day audience.

I have never seen better pantomimes than Conquest produced at the Surrey, when Dan Leno played there. It was George Conquest who released Dan Leno to Augustus Harris at Drury Lane Theatre.

If it is possible to pick out any of his brilliant make-ups rather than others, I would mention his "Nix, the Demon's Head," in which he appeared as a huge and ugly head without any body. The contortions and grimaces he contrived with this queer "face" were astounding. Then one time he made up as a tree, which came to life magically - a clever and realistic prop which no one could see without admiring its mechanical perfection, not to mention the skill with which it was "worked."

Another amazing piece of acting was his "Old Man of the Sea" in "Sinbad the Sailor." Here he had worked out a particularly effective and ingenious entrance. Sinbad, fishing off the harbour, hooks out a large bottle. The bottle smashes on the stage and out jumps this extraordinary apparition, the real "Old Man of the Sea."

Arthur Conquest, the youngest member of the Conquest family, even took me in with a make-up he had as a chimpanzee. I went one night to the Kingston Empire to see Wee Georgie Wood in a revue, and Georgie brought a chimpanzee on to the stage by a chain attached to a belt around the "animal's" waist. The "business" that Wee Georgie did with the chimpanzee was very startling, and I wondered as I watched whether it was safe for him to play about with the animal without the trainer being present.

When the performance was over, I went round to see Georgie in his dressing room.

"That's a marvellous chimp you've got, Georgie," I said, "but I shouldn't like to play about with it the way you do on the stage. If it turns on you....."

Georgie laughed. "You know him, don't you?"

"Know him" I asked. "How do you mean?"

"Why, it's Arthur Conquest."

I was honestly surprised. And I - an old pro who had played monkey myself many times - had actually been deceived by his performance! Many times since then I have had Arthur playing in companies I have been running, when he was generally introduced by his clever little daughter Betty, and rarely did I miss an opportunity of being at the side of the stage myself to watch his act.

When this Wimbledon pantomime ended I went into a musical play called the "Apache" for a year, and then came an offer to play the principal comedy part in a new all-British musical comedy called "Lumber Love."

The show opened on January 23, 1928, at the Prince of Wales Theatre, Birmingham. It broke all records the theatre had made for thirty-seven years, and wherever we went in the provinces it was the same. We smashed the gate. Yet, when it came to London, it only ran for sixteen weeks.

However, Mr. James Agate gave us a whole column in the "Sunday Times" when we opened at the Lyceum, and slated and praised and satirised to the length of a thousand words or more, - a compliment he does not pay many musical comedies.

I hope I won't be accused of being too proud of myself if I pick out some phrases from his article that were particularly gratifying to me: "For the rest, the piece is good only when it stops being a piece and allows Mr. Fred

Kitchen to come on and be funny.... The success of this piece.... is due to two things: these are the music and Mr. Fred Kitchen..."

Then this eminent critic pays me the further compliment of revealing that he has discovered the secret of my work. He has put into words my own beliefs:

"There is much to be said for the provinces, that they will not be put off with the appurtenances and the gadgets of the professional funny fellow, but insist on the body of fun itself... the clown who can make Lancashire laugh today can be sure of making London laugh for any number of tomorrows. But Mr. Kitchen, beloved of Lancashire and the North, though he content himself in this piece with mere clowning, is ever so much more than a buffoon. He is an actor, an actor possessed, moreover, with an extraordinary gift of pathos; and it should be written over every comedian's door that *only the player who at a pinch can make an audience cry, can make an audience laugh...*"

The italics are mine, for that, I think, neatly sums up the whole secret of my success.

* * * * *

For the rest, I have little to tell that would not be a repetition of what I have already written, but for names and dates; but I must just mention my essay into the Film world.

It was a couple of years ago that Albert de Courville invited me to come along and have a film test for a talkie he was producing. It was merely a small part with Binnie Hale and Gordon Harker that he used for the test, but he liked the result well enough to cast me for the part of the trainer in his "Mick the Miller" film, - "Wild Boy", - which was released a year later.

Now I have come to the end of my story. I have tried to describe in proper proportion my successes and my failures, my good times and my bad. On the whole I have been lucky, and I have done my honest best to deserve my luck. I have had the good fortune, I believe, to strike the right note to provoke the healthy laughter of the land. I have been helped on every side by my fellow artistes of both sexes and all ranks, and by the managements and staffs of the scores of theatres and music halls where I have played, and most of all by the public who pay to be entertained.

I am intensely grateful for all the help and the friendship that have been extended to me in a thousand places, and in ten thousand ways, on my long and adventurous journey. From the days of old-fashioned Melodrama and Pantomime to the era of "Talkies" and Greyhound Racing, - from the "Dumb Man of Manchester" and Harlequinade to the Film Studio and "Wild Boy."

Said a young friend to me recently: "You must have had a wonderful life, Mr. Kitchen."

"Yes," I said, "I think I have."

Epilogue

After a long and successful career Fred retired from the stage in 1945. The profession gave him a farewell benefit at the Winter Garden Theatre, London, on 9th December. Well-known stage people were on the bill and as a result a cheque for £2000 was presented to Fred by his fellow-pros.

He continued to meet them and talk shop at the gatherings every other Sunday at the Eccentric Club, meeting place of the Grand Order of Water Rats of which he was one of the oldest members.

His beloved wife, "Nell", died in 1941. Fred continued to live in South London until his death after a short illness on April 1st 1951. He is buried in the family grave in West Norwood Cemetery, and yes, his headstone is engraved with the words "Meredith, we're in"!

WINTER GARDEN THEATRE
DRURY LANE, W.C.2

Licensed by the L.C.C. to MILLENNIUM PRODUCTIONS LTD.
Lessees ... ... MILLENNIUM PRODUCTIONS LTD.
Direction ... ... MALA de la MARR & JACK HYLTON

SUNDAY,
DECEMBER 9th, 1945
at 6.30 p.m.

Complimentary
BENEFIT
to
FRED KITCHEN

PROGRAMME

Printed in Great Britain
by Amazon.co.uk, Ltd.,
Marston Gate.